washed by blood

also by brian welch

save me from myself

washed by blood

lessons from my time with korn and my journey to christ

brian welch

HarperOne

An Imprint of HarperCollinsPublishers

All scripture citations have been taken from the New International Version (NIV) of the bible.

I have changed the names of or used nicknames for some individuals, in order to preserve their anonymity. The goal in all cases was to protect people's privacy without damaging the integrity of the story.

HarperCollins books may be purchased for educational, business, or sales promotional use. For information, please write: Special Markets Department, HarperCollins Publishers, 10 East 53rd Street, New York, NY 10022.

Designed by Ralph Fowler / rlf design

FIRST EDITION

Library of Congress Cataloging-in-Publication Data is available upon request.

ISBN: 978–0–06–155580–0

08 09 10 11 12 RRD(H) 10 9 8 7 6 5 4 3 2 1

To my two best friends:

the Holy Spirit and my daughter, Jennea.

I'm forever grateful to both of you

for saving me from an early grave.

They overcame him by the blood of the Lamb

and by the word of their testimony.

—Revelation 12:11

contents

part two

god finds me

author's note

My life. What a trip it's been so far. Like most people, I've had enough ups and downs in my life to drive me crazy. Like most people, my heart has been beaten up pretty badly throughout the years by myself and by others. Like most people, many of the things that I've chased after in my life have left me feeling empty and unsatisfied.

Unlike most people, I had a childhood dream to become a rock star that came true. I was able to do what I wanted to do, go where I wanted to go, and buy what I wanted to buy. Unlike most people, I gave all this up—my music, my band, my career, everything—when I had an encounter with God. After that, all I wanted to do was focus on my future, sweeping everything from my past away and moving on with my new life. Or, at least, that was my plan until a friend suggested that I write a book about my life.

At first, I didn't know how I felt about that. I didn't know if I wanted to dig up all the painful memories from my past, because they were just that: the past. As a new follower of Christ,

I had been undertaking the process of crucifying my past and starting a new chapter in my life. I mean, why would I want to *relive* the past if I'm trying to forget it?

Well, I prayed about it, and after a lot of thought, I came to the conclusion that exposing the darkness from my past would be part of my healing process. I also came to see that discussing some of the stupid things I've done might save a lot of people from going down the same roads of destruction that I traveled on. It was with this goal of helping others that I decided to write my story, to share some of my inner demons with others, so that perhaps you or someone you know can avoid the trouble that I came to know all too well. That's my heart's intention, anyway. Don't get me wrong—my past wasn't all bad. I had some good times, but most of those always seemed to lead me into trouble.

Another reason I really wanted to write this book is to help explain to my family, friends, and fans how I came to this major decision to drop everything and follow Christ. You see, I was a master at hiding my pain and anguish from absolutely everyone. I was always the one who made everyone laugh—everyone except myself that is. I would always act like a goofball, appearing to be a normal, happy guy when I was around people. But it was all a front to cover up the prison that my heart was in. Behind closed doors, I was a very depressed, lost soul. As you read this book, please remember that while my outer life looked happy to the rest of the world, there were a lot of things happening inside me that no one knew about. This is the story of that inner life.

You're also going to read about how God has taken every bad thing I went through and turned it around for good. That's just what he does. I've been completely clean and sober for over three years; my life has never been happier.

And if he did it for me, he'll do it for anybody.

I hope this book touches your heart in some way.

part one

life without god

1. in the beginning

I grew up in a southern California town called Bakersfield, about an hour and a half from Los Angeles. In the past few years, the place has grown a ton, but when I was younger, it was still pretty small. There are two important things you should know about Bakersfield when I was younger:

- It was hot (we pretty much baked in the heat every summer, so we started calling it Bako).

- There wasn't much to do.

My childhood there was pretty typical. Like a lot of kids in Bako, I grew up in a nice enough house with nice enough parents. We were pretty much a typical middle-class family of the 1980s, living at the end of a cul-de-sac in a one-story house with a basement. The basement was everyone's favorite room. We had a home theater system down there (well, as good as

---

This photo was taken when I was about five. Even then I had a habit of making a mess.

home theaters got back then), huge couches, a huge pool table, a big Asteroids game (just like they had at the arcade), and some workout equipment. Even my dad liked hanging out down there, since that's where he had his wet bar and a little bathroom he used every morning to get ready for work.

Because both of my parents worked a lot in order to provide for me and my older brother, Geoff, there wasn't a lot of time for hugs in the house. While I knew we all loved each other, it wasn't the kind of place where everyone said it or showed it all the time. We didn't talk about feelings and we didn't go out of our way to comfort each other. For the most part, my dad was a pretty cool guy. He coached my soccer team as well as my brother's, took us motorcycle riding, and when he was in a good mood, he made us laugh a lot.

But every now and then, he'd have these moments when he'd get kind of crazy. I don't want to sound like I grew up with some abusive father or anything, because he wasn't; when he was nice, he was really nice. But when he got angry, he got scary. Part of it had to do with his drinking; his dad was an alcoholic, and my dad drank a bit too.

While my dad usually got happy when he was drunk, he definitely had his moments when his temper would flare up—even over little things. I remember a few times when my brother or I would spill a glass of milk at dinner, and he'd change into a totally different person, yelling at us with a voice full of anger, a voice that made us feel like we were going to get beatings, though he never followed through with those. A few minutes after his anger fits ended, he was usually back to normal. They were scary moments, but then they would pass.

Mostly, though, my dad drank to escape things. His mother died when I was in high school, and his drinking got much worse after that. I remember one time I came home in the middle of the day and saw that my dad had stopped by to pick up some papers. When I came into the kitchen, he was sitting there with a glass of water in front of him. I was about to take a swig when I realized what it really was: vodka. Drinking became how he dealt with things, and it didn't do much to stop his outbursts of anger.

My mom didn't have the same problem with drinking and, for the most part, she was pretty cool and laid back—more or less your standard mom. She was a good cook, made dinner every night, helped get us ready for school in the mornings, kept the house really clean, basically your typical mom stuff. A lot of the time, it seemed like she had it more together than anyone else in our house, but she had her issues too—just like everyone else in the world. Growing up, I felt the most love from my mom, probably because she didn't have the unpredictable emotions that my dad did.

My brother Geoff is two years older than I am, and, like all brothers, he and I fought a lot when we were kids. A couple of times it was brutal, but it wasn't always that way. We also used to play games together for hours and make each other laugh. As we got older and became teenagers, we began pushing each other away in a more serious manner. In general, it wasn't personal; it was mostly that we were just into different stuff.

For example, I was into heavy metal (think: AC/DC), but he was into new wave music (think: Duran Duran). Back then the rockers didn't get along with the new wave crowd. Geoff used to pin his jeans real tight at the bottom, and his hair was long on one side of his face—down past his eye—while on the other side, it was cut short; it was the classic new wave hairdo. I would constantly make fun of him for it and for being new wave in general.

One time we were arguing in our basement about something stupid, and I picked up a pool cue and whacked him with it as hard as I could. Got him good too. I knew he was going to kill me for that, so I ran to my mom and hid behind her until he calmed down. Even though he didn't get me that time, he usually got me back. When he was sixteen, he had this yellow Volkswagen bug that was slammed to the ground with matching yellow rims. One day I took the bus a half hour across town to go hang out at the mall all day with one of my friends, and at the end of the day, I was tired and seriously not looking forward to another half hour bus ride home. We saw my brother in his bug, and I asked him for a lift.

"No way!" he said. "I ain't giving a ride home to no *rocker*."

Like I said: different.

Our family moved from Los Angeles to Bako when I was in the fourth grade. My dad decided to go into business with my mom's brother, Tom, and his wife, Becky, and together they ran a Chevron truck stop in East Bakersfield, managing a staff of full-time truck mechanics, gas pumpers, and cashiers. My mom also worked with my dad at the Chevron.

Looking back on it, it was amazing that the two of them got along so well. They worked together all day, five or six days a week, then came home at night and dealt with Geoff and me. They had their problems—and we added to them—but they worked hard to make money and to make us a family.

My parents' house in East Bakersfield was a three-minute walk from my school, Horace Mann Elementary, which was the oldest school building in Bako. One morning on the way to school, I met a group of kids who lived nearby and we started hanging out after school, mostly in my parents' basement because it was so tricked out. While my parents didn't love having my friends over all the time, at least that way they knew I wasn't getting into trouble. East Bakersfield had a real problem with gangs back then, not so much gun-toting bangers, but a lot of guys who got into fights with knives and fists. I wasn't a fighter, so I picked up a guitar instead.

metal begins

I became interested in music around 1980 when I was ten years old, roughly a year after we moved to Bakersfield. My parents' very good friends (and my godparents), the Honishes, were big influences on me. Frank, my godfather, was a guitar player, and they had a piano in their house that I always liked to plink on. Even then, there was something about playing music that fascinated me, so when I saw Frank play his guitar, I started getting interested in learning an instrument myself.

The funny thing is that I originally wanted to play drums, but my dad talked me out of it. I remember him telling me, "You don't want to haul around a drum kit all the time." I think he just didn't want to listen to me banging on the drums all the time in his house. What he didn't count on was that I would get into heavy metal and crank up my guitar all the time. Either way it was going to be loud. He thought he was doing himself a favor, but he had no idea how loud it would get.

With drums out of the question, I chose a guitar—not just any guitar, a Peavey Mystic. Have you ever seen one of those? If you have, you know exactly the kind of music I was into. If you haven't, go track down a picture on the Internet. It's maybe the most metal-looking guitar ever made.

My whole family was really supportive of my new obsession, and my mom even started taking me to lessons every week. After a while, I pretty much understood what was going on with the whole guitar thing. I wasn't a metal guitar hero or anything, but I had a good ear, so it made sense and came pretty naturally. Playing for me was just something that happened, like someone had kind of blessed me with this ability. I worked hard at it and practiced it all the time, but it came to me at just the right moment. I don't think I knew it then but I was searching for something to be good at, something to help me focus my life.

When I found the guitar suddenly I had that. It was like someone had finally told me I was doing something right.

The more I played, the more I could hear where notes were
supposed to go, and about a year after I started playing, I began
teaching myself Ted Nugent, Queen, and Journey songs. While
those were fun, what made me get really psycho over playing
guitar was when AC/DC's *Back in Black* album came out. I
remember hearing it and thinking, *I want to be just like Angus
Young!*

That album made me dive into my guitar. Here I was, close
to being a teenager, not too good with my parents, but really
good on this guitar—I started playing constantly. My parents
took an interest in my playing too. Sometimes they'd come into
my room and listen while I practiced. Even Geoff would take
his new wave friends into my room and have me play Eddie
Van Halen's guitar solo called "Eruption." He was proud of his
little rocker brother, even if he didn't want to give me any rides
in his car. It was fun just to play. From an early age, I loved
playing music. Loved it. The guitar became a huge part of my
identity. Others were admiring my skills—like it was what I was
born to do.

And I loved metal. Iron Maiden, Ozzy, Judas Priest, Mötley
Crüe, Van Halen—all that stuff—and I had the look to prove it.
As far as looks were concerned, I was living the metal lifestyle.
I had a huge collection of pins from my favorite bands, and I'd
pin them on everything: shirts, hats, and my favorite jean jacket.
My mom taught me how to use her sewing machine, and I even
started sewing the legs of my pants to make them skintight so I
could tuck them into these big, white-top tennis shoes I wore.
With all that stuff—plus all my metal T-shirts—I was completely devoted to metal music.

I guess you could say it was my religion.

drug dabbling

When I was a little bit older, I met this kid named JC, and we were kind of bad for each other. Most of the time when we hung out, we just spent the hours listening to metal music. He played the drums and I played guitar, and we'd jam in that basement in my house, or in his garage. I don't think we ever came up with a name for our band, probably because we really didn't have a band. It was just the two of us.

But sometimes we'd smoke cigarettes or roll parsley joints with brown paper bags while my parents were at work. Once in a while we smoked real weed too. As I got older, marijuana made occasional appearances in my life. I didn't smoke much of it in high school, mainly because when I was a freshman, I had the craziest experience with it that scared me off drugs for the next few years.

I was at my friend Paul's house, when he told me his cousin had just gotten some really good weed, and now he had some of it. He showed it to me, and I could see that it had these little crystals or something in it. But the crystals didn't bug me, so I bought a couple joints, stashed them, and then went home one day after school to try one of them out. My parents were at work, so I headed to the backyard by our pool, pulling up a chair, and checking the clock, just to make sure I had enough time to get baked, then get over it before Mom and Dad were home.

Two thirty. Perfect. I lit up one of those crystallized joints, took a couple hits, and put it out.

Instantly, I no longer knew where I was.

Also, I could not move.

But I was sure my arms were melting off my body.

Since I couldn't move, I couldn't panic, which was probably a good thing because I was so close to the pool. This went on for a couple of minutes, and it was genuinely frightening, because I just *knew* I'd lost my arms, and then how was I going to play guitar?

And then I heard my dad's car pull up to the house. This was odd, his coming home so early in the afternoon so, with some effort, I turned my head to look at the clock.

Six fifteen? I'd been high for *four hours*? It only felt like a couple of minutes, but I had sat there, in my backyard, holding a half-smoked, unlit joint in my hand and staring at the ground for four hours straight. All while my arms were melting off. And then on top of it all, I had to go out to Sizzler that night—before the buzz had worn off—to have dinner with my family. That was a huge battle: looking them in the eye and talking to them, pretending I wasn't still high. I was so high, I didn't even have the munchies so I couldn't eat much of anything. Just faked it.

It wasn't fun at all.

With episodes like this, I was definitely heading down some wrong roads in life at an early age, but still, I managed to do things without my parents catching me. I guess that was part of the thrill too, but I don't know what my dad would've done if he found out what I was up to back then. He probably would've killed me.

picked on

In truth, my dad's tendency to fly off the handle over little things really affected me when I was in junior high. The anger in his voice put a fear in me that I carried around all the time, which eventually became a fear of confrontation. Because of that fear, I'd kind of cower at school when kids would mess with me.

I didn't walk around afraid all the time, but I did feel—and look—a little weak. When any of the bigger kids wanted to pick on me, I'd just let them. That fear of confrontation would kick in, and I wouldn't even defend myself. I was a wimp.

My worst memories of getting picked on were during the years when I was in middle school and junior high. My junior high was called Compton Junior High, and after school I would hang around with these two guys. They were pretty mean to me, and they used to hold me down and give me Pink Belly (they'd smack my belly with an open hand until it turned pink) until I would cry. Or they would simply hit me until I cried. Then they would feel bad and say they were sorry, but within a week, they were doing it again.

I hated not being able to defend myself against them, but I couldn't go running to Mommy and Daddy. Though I knew Geoff had my back, I couldn't let my big brother fight all my battles either. The result was that I was totally stuck in my own fear.

Because of that paralysis, I started acting out when I was alone at home. Sometimes I'd go get April, the family dog, bring her into my room, lock the door, and beat her with my fists. Now someone else was the wimp; *I* was the tough guy.

I also would have all sorts of evil fantasies about getting even with those guys at school. I'd picture the three of us at school when no one was around, playing hide-and-seek. And then in my fantasy, I'd pull a knife out of my pocket and stab them until they cried, just like I did.

I don't know why, but I continued to hang out with those two guys throughout junior high even though they picked on me. It didn't help that I was kind of little. (That's where I got my nickname, by the way. Those guys said my head looked like it was too big for my body, and so they started calling me Head. I guess it stuck. It seems funny now, but at the time it really made me sad. I walked around feeling like a big-headed freak.)

meeting kevin

With that kind of darkness going on in my life, it was clear that junior high was not the best time for me. To say I fell in with the wrong crowd is an understatement. I was hanging out with guys who picked on me, watching movies I shouldn't have been, and just generally messing up. The only thing that I loved was playing guitar. Beyond that, everything else was one big frustration.

The summer after my depressing junior-high career ended, I met a kid named Kevin who seemed pretty cool—in a goody-goody sort of way. He never made fun of me or beat me up the way my other so-called friends did. But that wasn't the only thing that was different about him. In general, he just wasn't like the other people I knew. It didn't take long for us to become best friends. During that summer between junior high and high school, we hung out a lot. We'd go ride motorcycles in the desert, he'd come over to my house and swim, or I'd go over to his house and jump on his trampoline.

The thing with Kevin was that his family lived in this little house, just down the street from mine, but even though his house was small, his entire family got along. Maybe it was because their house was so small and they couldn't get away from each other that they learned to be close. It was just so different from my family. We lived in a big house, and around that time we weren't getting along so well. If someone had put us in Kevin's tiny house, we probably would have killed each other.

But Kevin's family was always happy, always hanging out together and having a fun time, as a family. They actually seemed to like each other and to like me too. So I started hanging out there, and whenever I was there, I felt at peace. Whereas my house felt tense, his house was really calm and relaxed. What kid *wouldn't* go hang out at a peaceful place?

There was another thing about Kevin and his family: they talked about Jesus a lot. This didn't strike me as weird, but I don't know why, since no one else I knew back then ever talked about Jesus. I don't remember Kevin's family going to church—well, I never went with them, anyway—but they would talk a lot about Jesus while I was around. I guess going to a church building every Sunday wasn't as important to them as having a relationship with Jesus at home.

I never questioned it, or asked them more about it. I accepted it as part of who they were and what they did. My "friends" from junior high probably would have picked on Kevin like they'd picked on me, but I appreciated that he was part of a happy family that seemed to get along. That was their thing. I didn't know anything about Christians or God or Jesus. My only religious experience was when some priest sprinkled water on my head in an Episcopalian church when I was about three. When my brother and I were a little older (but still little kids—I think I was five), my mom tried to take us back to church for a few months, but we didn't really like Sunday School, and my dad didn't want to go, so that pretty much ended my religious experience. I didn't know how it all worked. I didn't know what any of this Christian stuff that Kevin and his family talked about meant.

Still, if all the talk about Jesus made their house a peaceful place for me to hang out, so be it, but Kevin also talked about Jesus when he was at *my* house. Since we lived close to each other, he'd come over to spend the night, and I'd try to get him to watch horror movies like *Friday the 13th*, but all he'd want to do was talk about Jesus. He'd just tell me about Jesus while I was watching Jason hack up a bunch a people.

That's just the way it was that summer. Before I met Kevin, I had been playing the guitar constantly, but during those months,

I didn't play as much since I was too busy hanging with Kevin and his family. I still played, but it wasn't the outlet it had been. I had a different outlet now.

Then came the fateful day that Kevin's mother laid everything out for me. I was over at Kevin's house, just hanging out in the family room and talking to his mom, when she flat-out said, "Jesus Christ is the savior of the world, and if you ask Jesus into your heart, he will save you and come and live inside of you."

I didn't understand. I was thirteen, with no religious or spiritual background, and this woman was telling me about some guy coming and living inside of me. I had no idea what she meant, but she explained it all so gently and with so much love, I thought I'd give it a shot, because here's what I knew: I liked these people, they were nice to me, and I felt happy when I was with them.

I didn't say anything to Kevin's mom right then, or pray with her, but that night after I went home, I couldn't shake the idea of what she'd said. I was sitting by myself in the basement, trying to watch a horror movie, and I couldn't get her words out of my head. I just felt drawn to the idea of Jesus, and when I thought about it, I felt a peace and love inside me I'd never felt before. It wasn't an overpowering feeling and it wasn't all that strong, but still, it was there.

I was unsure if what she had said about Jesus was true. After thinking about it, I decided it was better to be safe than sorry, so just in case, I went ahead and prayed to Jesus. I went downstairs into the cramped basement bathroom that always smelled like my dad's shaving cream and, kneeling down on the tile, I said, "Jesus, will you please come into my heart?"

I felt something.

I was thirteen years old; I didn't know what I was feeling, but I definitely felt something inside me change. What was I supposed to do about that? What changed? Was I supposed to change how I lived? I didn't know what to do, and my knees were getting cold from the tile, so I got up and pretty much went on with my life. I didn't know it at the time, but something had been set in motion in my life, something that I wouldn't experience for another twenty years or so.

Looking back on it now, it's clear to me that God reached out to me through Kevin. Kevin was a sign to help me see the alternate path. He saw that I was hanging out with the wrong people and doing things that weren't good for me, and he tried to get me to make the right choices. The only problem was I missed the signal, and it would be close to two decades before I would finally understand his message.

About a month after that experience, my first year of high school started. I stopped hanging out at Kevin's house and drifted back into my old ways. Kevin and I ended up going in different directions, and I didn't tell him—or his mom—about that night in the bathroom when I invited Jesus into my heart. I don't know why, exactly; I just never got around to it. By the time school started, Kevin and I were no longer really friends, and I started hanging out with some new people. I went hard back into my music, straight into metal.

Just like that, I was living my old life again.

With God and Kevin out of the picture for the time being, all I really had was my guitar and music, and I was completely committed to both. The guitar offered an escape from my problems, a way to cope with whatever I was going through—whether it was problems with the bullies at school or problems at home. I'd dream about becoming a rock star and playing for people all around the world, and suddenly I wasn't the kid getting picked on at school. I was larger than life. What I didn't realize at the time was that the guitar couldn't solve everything. As much as I wanted to believe that it held all the answers, I still had a lot of questions.

Though my life during junior high was a steady routine of practicing the guitar and hanging out with the wrong crowd, I finally got sick of those guys who made fun of me and I decided to do something different. I graduated junior high and was going to make a change with my life and start hanging out with different people. What I didn't know then was that those people would end up becoming Korn.

DISCUSSION QUESTIONS

1. Describe your relationships with your siblings (if you have them). What are your main areas of conflict? As a Christian, what's the best way to handle these tense situations?

2. Describe your parents' attitudes toward jobs/careers. If they work a lot, would you rather they worked less and spent more time at home? If so, how would you feel if that meant having fewer "toys" to play with?

3. Head discovered his biggest skill early on—playing the guitar. What's the one thing you're best at? Does it get you positive attention? Do you ever feel as though others like you (or use you) because of that skill?

4. Head admits that he was totally devoted to metal music when he was growing up. Is there something in your life that you're devoted to? Do you ever find yourself loving that object of devotion more than God? If so, how does that make you feel? How do you think God feels?

5. Are drugs a big temptation in your school or neighborhood? Do you know anyone who uses them? If so, what can you do to help that person?

6. Head describes his dad's anger episodes and how they negatively affected him. How do you respond when your parents (or others) get angry at you? Are they usually just trying to make a point—or does it sometimes scare you a little? What kind of ways can you improve communication with your parents?

7. Is fighting/bullying/getting picked on a problem at your school? How do you respond when others act immaturely in this way? Can you think of a Bible verse that talks about what we can do as Christians in these situations? (Hint: It's in the Gospel of Matthew.)

2. cars, girls, and rock bands

Within two or three years of starting high school, I was hanging out with almost all of the guys who would eventually form Korn. It would be quite a while before we became one of the biggest rock bands on the planet, but our individual experiences during our high school years played a big role in making us the band we would become.

A couple years into high school, I began spending time with a guy named Reggie Arvizu, who wound up being very important to my life. Reggie had gone to Compton Junior High with me, but I hadn't really been close friends with him. We were more like acquaintances, not really hanging out with each other, but talking every now and then. I used to tell him that Duran Duran was no good, and that he needed to quit listening to junk like that and get into groups like Ozzy and AC/DC.

This guitar wasn't the legendary Peavy Mystic. It was an Ibanez Explorer. Back then, it didn't even cross my mind that one day I would be endorsed by Ibanez.

While I was off doing my own thing in junior high, Reggie had hung out with a kid named Jonathan Davis, who I sort of knew as well. Jonathan also went to Compton, and sometimes after school, he and Reggie would hang out. Reggie had this three-wheeler ATV, and he was crazy on that thing. One day when Reggie was riding around, he accidentally ran over Jonathan. (Well, it depends on who's telling the story as to whether it was an accident—Jonathan always says it was intentional.) Anyway, if you can call running someone down on an ATV hanging out, then they hung out.

When high school came around, Jonathan and Reggie wound up going to Highland High School, while I went to East Bakersfield High. We lost touch for a bit, but during my sophomore year, I ran into Reggie at a party and cemented my friendship with him. I was only fifteen, and since I couldn't drive, my mom would drop me off at this sound company on Friday nights. She thought she was dropping me off to play guitar with my friends—but I was really going to these little parties they'd throw there. I didn't play my guitar; I just drank and listened to music. It was at one of those parties that I bumped into Reggie, and since we were both rockers now, we started hanging out all the time.

freedom on wheels

Not long after I started spending time with Reggie, I got my first true taste of freedom and the responsibility that comes with it. I wasn't even sixteen yet, but my dad told me that he would buy me any car I wanted as long as it cost less than three thousand dollars, was in good condition, and had low miles.

Well, my imagination started running, and I thought of how awesome I'd look in a Baja bug, with those big ol' fat tires in the back, and one of those huge, loud engines with all the pipes and stuff coming out. Oh, I wanted one so badly. In the end, we figured it'd eat up too much gas, so I decided against it.

I got a Toyota instead.

Now, this wasn't just *any* Toyota—it was a white automatic Celica hatchback, bought from a private seller in the newspaper. It was a good car, in good shape, and the price was right. And, the biggest deal of all—it was *mine*.

One problem, though: no stereo.

I guess it was kind of a good thing that I wasn't old enough to drive it yet, because having to drive without a stereo would've killed me. This way, I had plenty of time to work, save money, and get a stereo in there before I started driving it.

My dad's Chevron was always a go-to job for Geoff and me (and my cousins) whenever we needed money. So I talked to my dad about my need for cash, and he put me on at the Chevron to help me earn enough to buy that stereo. It went fine, too, until my hair got too long.

My hair was very important to me—I'd been growing it out since I was thirteen. It wasn't just a part of my image; it was a part of *me*. It was a part of the music I listened to and played, and if I was going to be true to myself and true to my music, I had to have the hair. But it was too long for Chevron standards, and I had to go get my own job.

Although I was busy looking for a job that would pay me enough to get the stereo and let me keep my hair long, I was still in love with that car. It was parked in my parents' driveway (since I didn't have my driver's license yet), and I would take a boom box out there and just sit in it for hours, blaring metal and cleaning the car up inside. It was like having another room that was just for me. My bedroom was cool, but it was in my parents' house. This room—the gray interior of the Celica—was my room, and having my own place was very important to me.

Finally, *finally*, I turned sixteen and set off in my Celica to take on the world. Or at least Bako.

pierct

Bakersfield had a few little rock bands that played around town, and Reggie was friends with all the cool rockers from those bands. Since I was friends with Reggie, that pretty much made me friends with them too. These guys were way older than we were—old enough to buy beer. We would all get together to hang out on the weekends and drink tons of beer, usually playing drinking games and listening to music.

While Reggie also played guitar, the only songs he knew how to play were "Freebird" and other stuff from the '70s because his dad and Jonathan's dad used to play that type of stuff around town. He showed me some of those classics, and in return I showed Reggie how to play more current songs. He wasn't that bad of a guitar player, actually, but he also wasn't that good. He just didn't have what it took to play in a band, so I said, "Man, you need to pick up a bass. There are less strings, and you can probably handle it better."

Now we just needed a drummer and a singer, and then we could be a full-on band. We tried out this kid named Jonny who supposedly played drums, but he couldn't keep a beat very well, so we fired him. After thinking about it for a bit, I called up my old friend JC from middle school; he agreed, and just like that, we had all the necessary instruments for a band.

The fact that we didn't have a singer didn't stop us. I started writing songs, with lyrics and everything, so we could be ready for someone to step in and pick up the mic. Writing songs and working with Reggie felt good. Suddenly I had a group of people who were as into music as I was, and playing was no longer a solitary thing. It was something I could do all the time with other people. For one of the first times, I belonged somewhere and my place was in a band. We rehearsed and rehearsed and rehearsed, and finally found this older dude named Ron to come sing for us. He was pretty good, so we let him stay.

We called ourselves Pierct. That's *pierced*, but we put a *t* on the end, because, well, just because. We practiced with Ron for a few months before we all felt ready to play for someone other than ourselves.

Reggie was really close friends with this older girl named Teresa, who had helped us get in with all those beer-buying rockers. She was pretty, and she had cool friends that she would let us hang out with. One of her friends was Jan, the unofficial rocker hairdresser for every band in Bakersfield. If you were in love with rocker hair, which I was, you had to have Jan take care of it for you.

Shannon was another one of Teresa's friends, and after I started driving, Teresa and Reggie hooked me up with her. I knew I was in love with Shannon on our first date. I had initially seen her when she was working at a fast-food burger place a few months before I asked her out. I came up to the counter and she had a look on her face that kinda said, "Well, what do you want?" as if she wasn't really happy to be working there.

I stumbled around placing my order, thinking the whole time about how cute she was (she had the whole "rocker" look down, like me) and figuring there was no way she would go out with me. Still, a couple months later, Teresa and Reggie told me she liked me, and I got up the nerve to ask her out. She was an awesome person, and I just knew we were going to be together for a long time.

Around that time, Teresa's boyfriend had a band that was pretty popular in Bakersfield, and she got us a gig opening for them. On the day of the show, we were incredibly nervous. The house was packed and expectations were high. Still, we came through and actually did pretty well. We went out there and played our original songs, some cheesy metal stuff with stupid song titles. The songs were terrible, but we actually sounded pretty good. The highlight of that show was our cover of U2's "Bullet the Blue Sky." The Edge has an awesome solo in that song, and I totally had it down to a T.

After that show, we were stoked to keep going, but we had a problem: Ron lived with his girlfriend and her kid, and he decided he couldn't be a rocker and a family man at the same time, so he quit the band.

And just like that, the life of Pierct was over—after one show.

When Ron left Pierct, Reggie, JC, and I tried to find some other guys to play with. After looking around for a bit, we lucked out by finding this band called Toy that consisted of a singer, Richard, and a guitar player, Tom. Toy had just lost their drummer and bass player, and we were exactly what they were looking for. They added JC and Reggie as a replacement drummer and bass player, and then just stuck me in as a second guitar player. That extra guitar had a great sound, and everyone really liked it. We had this rehearsal studio that we jammed in, and a lot of people used to come and listen to us jam sometimes, especially Shannon.

shannon problems

By this point, Shannon and I had been together for about a year. The two of us were really close, even though I was mean to her most of the time. She didn't deserve it.

I was very insecure, and that brought out the mean in me. When I was a freshman in high school, my face started to break out with some pretty bad acne, making me feel really ugly. My mom took me to our family doctor, which helped contain it a bit, but I could never fully get it under control until my late twenties. It completely devastated me, causing a lot of pain and anger that I took out on Shannon because I felt that whenever she stared at me she was looking at my acne. I just couldn't accept that she was staring at me because she loved me.

All I had to feel good about was my music, but that wasn't enough to take away all of the darkness I had inside of me. So I vented everything on Shannon and treated her horribly until one day, Shannon and I had a little scare. She was late with her period, and it really terrified us. I flipped. *She* flipped. It was all pretty heavy stuff for a couple of kids not yet out of high school. After about a week of uncertainty, we found out she wasn't pregnant, she was just late. Soon, we were back to the way we'd been before, and sadly, I was treating her badly once again.

I was also hanging with my new bandmates a lot. Those Toy guys were cool. We started drinking beer and hard alcohol while we practiced. It didn't take long for it to get out of hand, but I was sure I had it all under control. Altogether, Toy wasn't a bad band, except for this: just like Pierct, we played one show and then broke up.

I was so frustrated, just hoping to one day play in a band that could last for at least two gigs. I found real happiness being in bands, but that happiness kept getting snatched away, and I didn't understand why. Then JC split on us, which added to my frustration. While Reggie and I were just drinkers, JC had begun to mess around with drugs. He lost interest in playing drums and a lot of other stuff. At the time, we didn't understand it, and we thought it was stupid to be a druggie. But eventually, we would personally experience the way drugs can totally take control of lives.

So now, when it came to music, it was down to just me and Reggie.

looking for a drummer

While much of my anger came from drinking, insecurities, and my upbringing, another part of it stemmed from my musical frustration. Reggie and I missed playing in a band, and we wanted to get back on track and get a band going again. We put out the word that we were looking for a drummer. As we waited for a response, we just partied around town with our friends.

One day Reggie checked the answering machine at his house and heard this message from someone who sounded like a little kid. His name was David Silveria, and he said that he was a drummer and wanted to try out for our band. He said his mom could drop him off at our practices and then pick him up when we were done. Reggie was like, "Who's this little kid trying to be our drummer? He sounds like he's twelve."

Turned out that only his *voice* sounded like a little kid; we found out he was only a couple of years younger than us, so we decided to try him out. When we first met up with him at the studio, I looked at him and didn't expect much. He looked like a cross between Prince and the singer from Ratt. But when he beat the drums, he blew our minds. He knew how to play metal. We had our new drummer. We didn't have a singer, though. Or a name. We were also really missing the double guitar sound that we had in Toy, which got me to thinking about adding another guitar player that I knew from high school named James Shaeffer.

and another guitar player

I met James when I started high school. James wore brown moccasin boots and had this shaggy long hair—the typical dirthead rocker look. He played acoustic guitar a bit, and he'd come over to my house to watch me jam out on my electric guitar once in a while. I showed him a few things and, I guess inspired him to play, just like my godfather had done for me a few years earlier.

James only had an acoustic guitar, so after we'd been hanging out for awhile I sold him that Peavey Mystic, along with the amp. I bumped up the price and charged him more than what I paid, but that guitar looked awesome on him. Being from the same school and sharing a love for the guitar helped us to become good friends.

I knew that James's playing would be a great fit for our new group and it was. For a short while after that, my musical life revolved around Reggie, James, and David. We called ourselves "Russian Roulette," but we never ended up playing any shows because we never found a singer. Instead, we just rehearsed in David's mom's garage, practicing the same songs, over and over, with no vocals. It got pretty boring. We tried to write new songs, but it just wasn't happening, and we wound up giving up after a little while. Musically, we weren't clicking.

Reggie, James, and David went off together and started doing their own thing, writing songs in this style of music that I didn't really understand yet. They were listening to a lot of Red Hot Chili Peppers and Faith No More, so they started writing stuff like that, which I wasn't that into. I liked Faith No More's music, but I couldn't stand the singer, and I thought the Chili Peppers were just okay. I only liked the bass player, Flea. Reggie did too and that's when he started incorporating the slap bass technique in the heavy stuff they were writing, pretty much copying those two bands. Then they called up Richard from Toy, our old singer, and I have to admit—I felt left out. The thing I loved most—playing in a band—was taken away from me once again, and I became bitter and angry at whatever it was that kept me from doing what I wanted to do.

i wanted to die

I vented a lot of those and other suppressed feelings on Shannon, and after awhile, she started to turn on me. I don't know why, but when I treated her badly, it made me feel good inside, like I was scratching an itch inside me, like I felt when I was younger and I would hit April, our dog. I felt bad, but if I could make her feel worse, then I wouldn't feel as bad. It was wrong, and I knew it was wrong, but I didn't have a good sense of how I could do things differently. My anger, my aggression, my frustration, all these feelings would come pouring out, and with no outlet for them, I took it out on one of the people who loved me most.

Eventually, Shannon got sick of me and started to stand up for herself. The beginning of the end came one night when we got into a fight, and she started crying with her head down. I was drunk, of course, and I said, "Quit crying, you spineless jellyfish!"

And that did it. That right there. Something clicked inside her, and my doom was sealed. I was no longer the aggressive one. I was no longer in control of the relationship. I couldn't control her anymore, and I could feel her starting to pull away from me.

To add to the craziness, Reggie, James, and David moved to L.A. with their singer Richard and his mom Donna to try to make something of their music. We'd all graduated from high school by then (except David was only sixteen; David's mom gave him permission to move to L.A. to pursue music since he would be living with Donna), and they just got the hunger in their hearts to be in Los Angeles and to call their band "LAPD" (it stood for "Love and Peace, Dude").

It bummed me out, but I wanted to stay in Bako and try to make it work with Shannon. I loved her so much, and I regretted how I'd treated her. I just figured if I stayed around, she'd stay with me. It was looking shaky, though. She had enrolled at Bakersfield College and quickly started making new friends. One day I called her up and asked her to come over.

"I can't," she said. "I'm doing homework."

I heard someone else in the background—a guy's voice I didn't recognize.

"Who's there with you?" I shouted.

"Just my friend, from school," she said. "We're just doing homework."

I slammed the phone down and ran to my car. I was going to kill whoever this "friend" was. But by the time I got there, he was gone. Shannon didn't let me inside; she just talked to me while I was standing on her porch. She told me it was over for us. That was the first time I ever felt like my heart was getting ripped out of my chest. I had never loved someone before like I loved Shannon, and I had no idea how to deal with the loss of a relationship. It killed me.

In a way, I felt like Shannon hadn't left me; I felt like she died. One day she was there with me; the next she wanted nothing to do with me. I was eighteen years old and had just experienced what I thought was the worst thing that I would ever face in my life.

As I look back now and distinctly remember feeling those first thoughts of suicide that would become my companions down the road. My best friends moved away, and I lost my first love. I had nowhere to go, and no one to turn to. The most important people in my life had filled an emptiness inside me, but now they were gone. I had nothing to help me get through things. There was nothing that I could rely on, and it was almost like I had been abandoned by everyone, like there wasn't anyone that was looking out for me. All those dark feelings that I had been struggling to hide from suddenly found their way out, and I had no way to control them.

I wanted to die.

DISCUSSION QUESTIONS

1. Do you have your driver's license yet? If not, how important is it to you to have one? Do you imagine it will open up all sorts of doors to "freedom," like Head talks about? What kinds of freedom are you looking for?

2. Do you have your own car? Head compares having his own car like having his own special place, all his own. Is that how you feel about your car—or *imagine* you'd feel if you had one? Why is having a place to call your own important to you?

3. Are you in a band or other musical group? If not, how about a sports team? Or a club? Or a Bible study? Head's rock bands gave him a sense of community and belonging when he was growing up. Can you think of places in the Bible that talk about Christians needing each other?

4. Everyone wants a girlfriend or boyfriend—it's just a matter of *how much*. On a scale of 1 to 10 (with 1 being "not important at all" and 10 being "there's nothing as crucial!"), how important is having a significant other in your life? Where on the scale do you suppose God wants it to be?

5. Relationships are never easy, but sometimes things can get pretty bad, as Head describes in this chapter. Do you know anyone in a dysfunctional relationship? If so, what can you do to help that person?

6. Have you ever been hurt by people leaving you in some way? Head had a double whammy—at the same time, his first girlfriend and his band ditched him. How can a relationship with Jesus help in such a traumatic situation?

3. finding korn

I must have done a good job keeping all this stuff to myself, because it seemed that no one knew the pain I was carrying around inside. No one knew the depth of my depression. No one knew I wanted to die. The only thing my parents knew was that I was just out of high school and in need of a job. And they told me so. Quite a few times. And since I didn't have Chevron-approved hair, I couldn't just go work for my dad.

It seemed like all my parents cared about was me getting a job, but I needed them to care about me. My heart was completely broken, and all I really wanted was for my mom and dad to just hold me and tell me everything was going to be all right. I needed their comfort and their support, but because we didn't have a lot of hugs or communication in our house, I didn't know

High school rocker. This was why my new wave brother would never give me rides, but I didn't care. This photo was taken around the time that I started hanging out with Reggie in high school, when neither one of us had any idea of what was on the horizon.

how to ask for this. When it came to emotions, I didn't know how to speak with anybody. It seemed like I was getting rejected everywhere I turned—nothing stuck around, satisfied, or comforted me for very long, if at all.

Tired of the whole Bako scene and life with my parents, I drove out to L.A. to visit my friends, and they instantly saw how brokenhearted I was. They knew I needed them; well, Richard's mom, Donna, did anyway. She asked me if I wanted to get out of Bakersfield and move in with them. It was a huge step for me to move out of my parents' house, but Donna made me feel like she cared about my broken heart, and I was drawn to her compassion. Her reaction to my sadness was just so different from what I experienced from my parents. All I could think about was the fact that my parents weren't there for me, and now Donna and my friends would be. Plus I wanted to drink my pain away with all my friends. It all sounded very exciting and the whole idea gave me hope again, so I accepted the invitation.

A couple days later, I went home to grab my belongings and tell my parents I was moving out. When I arrived back at my new home in L.A., it seemed like the suicidal feelings had disappeared completely. But appearances can be deceiving. I started drinking every night of the week instead of just on weekends, and as a result my dark feelings didn't go away, they just burrowed underneath. I didn't put it together that I was dealing with my pain the same way that my father often dealt with his: alcohol. Instead, LAPD rehearsed constantly, and I hung out with them all the time, drinking while they practiced in a rehearsal space they'd rented in Hollywood.

Even though we were broke, Donna took care of us, but after a while, she got sick of us living with her. (What parent wouldn't get sick of living with a bunch of partying teenagers just out of high school?) There were two guys living in the living room, three guys in the bedroom, and Richard's mom in the master bedroom. That lasted about a year, but when Donna had enough of everybody, she and Richard moved to Redondo Beach. The rest of us moved to Long Beach to share the living room in James's dad's apartment and kept doing exactly what we'd been doing.

Our routine was the same every day: sleep during the day (we didn't have jobs to go to), get drunk on malt liquor every night. We would buy forties in Hollywood, and the band would just practice, playing a few shows every now and then. Sometimes we went out on Sunset Strip to pass out flyers for their shows. I never liked their music that much, but I liked hanging out with them and carrying their equipment, kinda being their roadie. After a while, LAPD (they had changed the meaning to "Laughing as People Die") got a deal with XXX Records, but it was hardly what anyone would call lucrative.

Basically, the label gave them just enough money to make a record and nothing else. Even so, a couple of them got attitudes when they got that record deal. One night, Reggie came home drunk, and from out of nowhere, he said to me, "I got a record deal. What are you doing with *your* life, you loser?" It sounds funny now, but it really hurt me at the time because we'd been best friends for so long. Another rejection from someone I cared about.

Plus, it was true. I *was* a loser. And that truth hurt even more.

back to bako

Life in L.A. had helped me to get over Shannon, but by then I was getting over L.A. too. After about a year there, everyone was starting to get on everyone else's nerves; plus, I was sick of being drunk and broke all the time. I started to think that I had to get away from these guys, especially Reggie, so I said to

James, "Dude, I gotta leave. I gotta go back home to Bakersfield and do something."

I really wanted him to talk me out of it, to say, "No, stay here, man."

Instead, he said, "All right. Later."

Hope faded again—I couldn't see then that all the things I had been relying on were failing me. I didn't understand why things never seemed to get better and only seemed to stay the same. I had no choice but to bail back to Bako.

When I got back home, I chilled out for a few months and did a lot of soul searching to decide my next step. Though I didn't really know what to do with my life, I did know that I wanted to do *something* with music as a career, so I went to my dad and asked him if he could help me out. He agreed and gave me some money to go to Los Angeles Recording Workshop to learn recording.

So there I was. It was 1990, I was twenty years old and headed back to L.A., this time by myself. It was kind of lonely and overwhelming, being out there with no friends, but I adjusted quickly; it became a good thing for me. While I was in school, I also stopped drinking, so that was even better. It was the first time in a while that I had really focused myself on something that wasn't drinking or my friends. It felt good; the only problem was that, like most things, it came to an end.

A few months later, I graduated and began looking for jobs at the many recording studios in L.A. There were jobs out there, but none of them paid anything. They all expected me to work for free as an intern before they'd hire me on as an employee, and I couldn't do that since I needed to support myself. I had a couple of roommates, but I still had bills to pay and stuff to buy. Working for free simply wasn't an option.

In the end, I took the only paid music industry job I could find: testing drum machines and effects processors for an electronics company. I hated that job. For months, all I did, all day long, was push buttons on these machines as they came off the assembly line to make sure all the buttons lit up. I worked that job for absolute minimum wage, made close to nothing, barely paid rent. My bosses were all jerks and treated all the employees like peons.

hanging with creep

In addition to taking this job, I also took up drinking again. I began to get unhappy with life, stuck in a rut, far from music, and depressed. Again. By that point, LAPD had broken up, and all the guys had moved down to Huntington Beach to get something else going.

I didn't know what they were up to, but I was so depressed that one day I called them and asked if they were still playing together. They told me they'd gotten another singer named Corey and were now calling themselves Creep. They told me to come hang out and party with them.

Hanging out with those guys, drinking, and being stupid, helped me push my depression down inside me to a place where I couldn't feel it anymore, to the same place I pushed all the other pain in my life. So I started hanging with them more and more. It wasn't long before David asked me to move in with him and our good friend Danny.

It sounded good to me, so I quit my job testing drum machines and took off for Huntington Beach—along with fifteen drum machines I'd stolen from the company (I told myself it was okay because my bosses had mistreated me, so they deserved it). When I got to Huntington, I put ads in the newspaper to sell those drum machines for two hundred dollars each. A few of the guys sold weed for a living, so I guess I fit right in selling stolen drum machines. I wound up living on that money for months, but I never felt good about it. I just did what I felt I had to do at the time.

Pretty soon, Danny, David, and I moved into a new place in downtown Huntington, where I lived in the front closet. I don't know if it was really supposed to be a closet or just a small office. It was just a tiny room with a window, a door, and enough room for a twin bed, my stereo, my guitar, and a small amp. There was about a foot of space along one wall that the bed didn't touch.

I also rigged up a bamboo partition a little bit outside, just to have a little more room, and in the bamboo, I cut a little doorway in it to make it look like an entrance. Inside the bamboo was a cardboard wardrobe box from a moving company where I hung all of my clothes.

James lived down the street with his girlfriend, Bridgette, and he came over to party with us all the time. By then, Reggie had gotten married, so we only saw him at band practice. After about a year in that apartment with Danny and David, my life began to get into as dull a routine as my job testing drum machines had been: work, listen to the guys jam, party, sleep.

In 1992, at the age of twenty-two, I decided I was done with the routine. For real. Once again, I was sick of being drunk and broke all the time, and once again, I decided to head back to Bako.

And once again, I called my dad for help.

"Dad, I don't want to live like this anymore. I need to do something with my life, and I was wondering if I could come work at one of your Chevron stations for you and maybe go to college or something."

"Sure, Brian. But only if you cut your hair."

"Okay."

That's how desperate I was. I had been growing my hair out for years, and I chopped it all off to learn the family business.

I didn't go back to Bakersfield right away, but I came up with a date for the move and got ready to head back. But then something crazy happened. Just four days before I was set to move, David asked me if I wanted to audition with Creep before I left.

"Come jam with us and see if two guitars would be cool," he said. "It might be a sound we want."

I had been hanging out with those guys for so long that I was pretty surprised by David's request. He didn't know it, but that's secretly what I had been wanting the whole time. I had started a couple of those guys on their instruments when we were younger, and I really missed jamming with them. Now they were inviting me to play with them again, and I was so excited, I can't even tell you. It was a great feeling.

On the night when we finally headed to their rehearsal studio for the tryout, I was so nervous. Not only was I rusty because I hadn't played in quite a while, but I didn't want to be disappointed. They were all my friends, but I had this fear that it wasn't going to work out. For so long I had been excluded from their playing, and now that I had a chance to rejoin, I didn't want it to slip away. I wanted to belong to their group. If they rejected me, it was going to destroy me.

The list of reasons for my nervousness kept growing: James played an Ibanez seven-string guitar, and I had never really played one of those before. (It has a low B string above the low E, and it gives the guitar a thundering bottom end.) My only experience was on a standard six-string guitar, which wouldn't have worked for Creep. So I borrowed one of James's guitars for our jam session, and though it took me awhile to get used to the fatter neck, I adjusted quickly enough.

When we eventually jammed, the sound was unreal. Huge. This huge, huge sound that blew us all away. It was incredible. I don't think any of us were expecting how perfect it would be.

They asked me right there to join the band for good, and I agreed. I was excited for so many reasons. I had played well, I was playing music with my friends again—just like the good ol' days in Bako. We all felt like I had the ear they needed to take them to that next level, musically. And finally I got to be in a band again—the one thing that made me happiest.

The first thing I did was call up my dad and tell him, "Thanks for the job, but I think I'm going to stay here and try this music thing for a little bit."

Despite the uncertainty of my life in L.A., I knew that staying put was the right decision. I had this emptiness inside me, a dissatisfaction that was eating at me, but I was sure that if I could become a successful musician, the emptiness would finally be filled.

Now that I was playing with my friends, life suddenly had meaning again.

DISCUSSION QUESTIONS

1. In Head's depressed state, he wanted his parents' comfort but didn't get it—plus he didn't know how to ask for their help. Do you ever feel this way? If so, how does God's promise to comfort us (2 Cor. 1:3–4) make you feel?

2. When Head joined his friends in L.A., he spent a lot of time drinking to mask his pain. Do you know anyone who drinks or drinks to excess? What are their reasons? Can you help them identify things in their lives they're trying to "heal" through drinking?

3. After Head got the gig playing guitar with his friends in Creep, he felt that "life suddenly had meaning again."

If God had wanted Head to become a Christian all along, why do you suppose he let him find things in the world that seemed to satisfy him early on in his musical career? What seemed to satisfy you before you came to Jesus?

4. the band

A few months before I joined Creep, the band met a producer named Ross Robinson, who went to a couple of their shows and really liked their sound. Ross wanted to help Creep because he saw a lot of potential there, so he hooked them up with a manager named Larry. Together, Ross and Larry did what they could to get Creep out there, even going so far as to pay for a demo to shop to record labels.

Not long after Creep invited me to join them, I played my first show with them in L.A., and it was a total blast. It was the third live show I had ever played and, just like I was addicted to alcohol, I was addicted to playing live. I had found my religion again. Suddenly all of the depression and the sadness, the boredom with my routine and the frustration with my life seemed to go away. I was playing live and playing with my friends, that was all I thought I needed.

It took a while for the band to come together, but when we did, it seemed like nothing could stop us. This photo was taken at the 1999 MTV Music Awards.

My roommate, Danny, was really into making movies, and we were concerned with making our live shows as tight as they could be, so we had Danny come out to the show to record our performance. After the show, David, James, and I went home and watched the video.

Then David said, "We're missing something. Should we get a new singer?"

I said yes before he finished the word *new*.

We called Reggie and told him what we thought, and after some conversation, we all agreed that the singer, Corey, had to go. It wasn't long before David called him up and broke the news to him. He was bummed and we felt bad, but we knew we had to do it if we were going to go anywhere.

So there I was: I had joined my third real band, played my third real show, and lost my third real singer. But I was just happy to be jamming with my friends again, so I didn't lose hope; I knew we would find another singer. One weekend James and I decided to head back to Bako for a few days to visit our families and party with some of our old friends from home.

We had no idea what we were in for.

scarecrow

In Bako, we wound up heading to this night club called John Bryant's, and there were a few bands playing there—nothing special, just the same ol' Bako rock bands. James and I were literally walking out the door when the last band started playing, so we stopped and headed back inside to catch one song.

The band had a skinny little twig for a singer, shaking with uncontrollable intensity. He was freaky. He looked like a stick figure—like a scarecrow. He was amazing to watch already, and he hadn't sung a note.

And then he sang.

James and I looked at each other, wide-eyed. This dude didn't have the best voice in the world, but the sound of it was like nothing we'd ever heard before. The rest of the band was pretty good too, but we felt they didn't have enough excitement and intensity in their music, so they didn't do this guy justice.

He was exactly what we were looking for.

We stayed for the rest of their set and were a little bummed when we left, wishing we could have a singer like that in our band. It turned out the singing scarecrow was Jonathan Davis, Reggie's old friend I knew from junior high. I hadn't even recognized him up on stage. When we got back to Huntington Beach, it wasn't long before we told Reggie and David about seeing Jonathan sing back in Bakersfield.

Right after we discussed it, David said, "Let's call him and tell him he needs to quit that band and move here to join our band." Somehow he got Jonathan's number and gave him a call. I remember all of us piling around David, trying to listen in as he told Jonathan, "You need to come join our band, come down here and check us out. Jam with us and see what happens."

Jonathan was flattered that we were so high on him, and he already knew Reggie—how could you forget someone who ran you over with a three-wheeler? And while he thought it was cool that we wanted him to come jam with us, he wasn't sure he should.

Jonathan was an assistant at the Bakersfield coroner's office, so he worked around dead people all the time and was into some weird, freaky things. In the end, he went to a psychic to find out whether he should come jam with us. The psychic told him that it would be beneficial for him to leave Bakersfield, move to L.A., and join the band. With that advice, he drove down to L.A. to meet us at Larry's office.

That meeting was a trip. Reggie and I instantly recognized Jonathan from Compton Junior High days. His face looked the same, but he had a big mop of dreadlocks on his head. He told us about going to see the psychic and how she told him that we would all be successful one day. He actually played us the tape of the psychic's reading. I don't know if I believed that the lady could actually tell the future, but it sure sounded good at the time.

The day after we met with Jonathan at Larry's office, we went to our studio in Anaheim to jam with him for the first time. The first song we played for Jonathan would later be called "Need To," and we could tell just from that song that our music was blowing his mind. He started trying to make up words to our music, right there on the spot.

We had this tiny PA, and we couldn't really hear what he was singing, so Reggie, James, and I walked over to the speaker while we played and put our ears right next to it to hear. When we finally heard his voice on top of our music, there were ear-to-ear smiles plastered on everyone's faces. We all knew he was the perfect match before we were even done jamming.

korn is komplete

Jonathan joined the band immediately. He quit his job at the coroner's office, grabbed his girlfriend, and they both moved in with me and David in Huntington Beach. I was tripping because I knew it was only a matter of time before we did something big. I felt like that psychic really did know how to tell the future, and I had a lot of confidence that we would get a record deal. Our new singer was good, our music was good, and we were only getting better.

Looking all the way back to LAPD, and even Toy, to an extent, none of the bands I mentioned ever really broke up—it was really always David, Reggie, and James with a different lead singer. But each time a new lead singer had come in, the band had changed names, and because of that tradition we decided we weren't going to call ourselves Creep anymore. Jonathan had an immediate idea for a new name. He suggested that we call the band Korn, and we all liked it. It sounded kinda creepy because it reminded us of the horror movie *Children of the Corn*.

With Jonathan on board and Ross producing, we started writing entirely new songs, and it was clear from the start that Jonathan was going to bring a whole dark edge to our songwriting. His vibe was to yell about the horrible childhood he'd lived through. Since I had my own set of issues stemming from my bully problems as a kid and the problems with my dad, I fit right in with him on that subject, as did the rest of the band.

We all felt connected in some way because most of us shared the same sort of pain when we were kids. The pain of being rejected, the pain of being picked on, the pain of not understanding our fathers' love for us. Every one of us had similar issues with our dads when we were kids. Our pain was one that a lot of our fans later shared. It felt good to be angry and vent through our heavy music. It felt like the music and our friendships were filling the void in our souls, and I assumed that it would only be a matter of time before success made us complete.

nicknames

We also decided that we needed nicknames, just to be a little different, and since we were spending so much time dwelling on our childhoods, we sort of reached back to those memories to come up with names. Three of us had nicknames that came from our friends making fun of our bodies' goofiness. I already told you about how I came to be called Head. Since this was the nickname I was known by for a long time before Korn started, I was stuck with it.

James has this really long pinkie toe that makes his foot look like it has a thumb on it, like a monkey's foot, so we called him Munky. He decided to spell it in a weird way, mainly just to be different. Reggie's first nickname, Gopher, started with me and a couple of friends back in Bako making fun of his big cheeks and big teeth. He obviously didn't like that, so we made up this word, *Gar*, and to us it meant "Gopher," so that's what we started calling him under our breath. But then he found out what *that* meant. He was kinda fat back then, so we added *-field* to the end of it and started calling him Garfield, like the overweight cartoon cat. Eventually, the *Gar* got dropped and we wound up calling him Fieldy.

Jonathan had a couple of nicknames, but they didn't last; neither did David's. So we just ended up calling them David and Jonathan. So there you go. Head, Fieldy, Munky, David, and Jonathan. In a band called Korn. With names like that, we *had* to be destined for greatness.

Larry, our manager at the time, hated the name Korn, by the way. He was convinced we'd never get a record deal with that name and that we needed to change it. We came back to him with our decision.

"Okay, Larry, we came up with another name. But if you don't like this one, we're going to use Korn."

Larry had red hair and a nice, big, kind of animated smile; he sorta looked like Ralph Malph from *Happy Days*. He smiled that big smile and said, "Cool, what's the new name?"

"We want to call the band Larry and put your face on the cover of our first album."

Larry's face turned bright red to match his hair. We laughed a little, and he joined in, and then said, "Fine, call yourselves Korn. But nobody's gonna sign you with that name."

I didn't think they would have signed us with the name Larry either, but whatever—at least he was wrong.

searching for success

All of us in the group devoted all of our time and efforts to succeeding. We were writing songs with Jonathan and coming up with great stuff, so it wasn't long before we had enough material to go back into the studio to cut another demo. Playing music and refining our sound consumed us, and we were hoping all of our hard work would pay off. When it was done, Ross and Larry started the whole shopping-the-demo-to-labels process all over again.

It was around that time when we also got our first gig, which went really well, and the crowd response was even better. We found a new practice space in Huntington Beach called The Underground Chicken Sound. It was owned by this dude we eventually called Ball Tongue, and almost immediately he began to take really good care of us.

Ball Tongue went nuts for us, actually.

He started setting up shows and printing T-shirts and stickers to use as promotion to sell at the shows. With his help, we tagged the whole city of Huntington Beach with our stickers—almost every traffic sign had a Korn sticker on it. As our fan base grew over the next year, he would also rent this big bus, throw a keg on it, and charge fans like twenty bucks to ride with us from Huntington Beach to L.A. We called it the Korn Party Bus.

Parties were also a good way to make a bit of extra money when things were tight. Sometimes we would get low on studio rent, so to make it up, we would buy a keg, set up at Underground Chicken Sound, and charge people around twenty bucks a head to come drink beer and watch us play. Ball Tongue would pass out fliers all over town, and it wound up being a decent way to make some money.

That dude was all over the place, all the time, doing all sorts of stuff for us. He never slowed down, and with so much going on, we started wondering where he got the energy to do everything. And then a couple of us found out how he was keeping up with all of it: speed (methamphetamines).

It wasn't long before I was right there with him.

the seeds of my addictions

It started one night after band practice. We'd all been drinking for a while and I was pretty drunk, so drunk that I didn't think I could make it home. I had done speed a couple of times with some friends back in Bako, so I knew that when you snorted it, it seemed to take away your drunkenness and make everything clearer. It also takes away your sleepiness. And then it takes your mind. And your body. And your soul.

I wish I had known that then.

Instead, all I knew was that I needed to sober up quickly. I grabbed some of Ball Tongue's speed and did a line so I could drive home. That's all it took, and I was hooked. After that night, I started doing speed about three days a week. Amazingly I kept the whole thing to myself. Speed is such a dirty drug, I didn't want anyone else to know I was using it. Ball Tongue and I would go score some on the sly, after band practice or some other time when the rest of the guys weren't around. It went on that way for a few months, until I found out something interesting: Munky was doing speed too. And guess what? So was Jonathan.

We were all doing it with Ball Tongue, keeping it to ourselves and doing it in secret. We each told Ball Tongue not to mention it to anyone else, so he never told on us. He just did it with us. Of course, once Jonathan, Munky, and I found out about each others' habits, we started doing speed together, and we got really into it. It was about that time when we came up with the name Ball Tongue (which became a song on our first album). Sometimes he would get so geeked out on speed that he couldn't talk, no matter how hard he tried. He would just sit there with his mouth open, tongue sticking out, and his tongue looked like it had a little ball on the end of it.

When we began doing speed as a group, it took us over because it jacked us up so much. We started trying to write music while we were all geeked out on speed, but a lot of the songs sounded stupid after we came down off the high and listened to them. A couple of the songs we kept though. One of them was a song called "Shoots and Ladders." Jonathan and I stayed up all night on speed coming up with that one. The lyrics were about children's nursery rhymes being evil. Another one was a song called "Helmet in the Bush." Jonathan and I wrote that song too. Oddly enough, the lyrics were actually about being addicted to meth and asking God to help us stop. Sadly that was one of the only times real prayer managed to work itself into our words in a positive way.

At first, snorting meth was fun, but I soon began to feel the effects of it, and my life started getting really evil. That's what the drug does. It sucks you in by making you believe you can quit at any time, but then you turn into an out-of-control monster. I would have these anger outbursts that were so violent, they scared me. Other times, I would get really confused. As if these problems weren't enough, I'd get paranoid to the point where I couldn't function properly.

It was messing with all of us in ways we never could have imagined. As for me, all my drug fears from the past were coming back to me, so one day, I gathered enough willpower and strength to quit. We all did—even Ball Tongue.

I slept for two straight weeks while I came down.

DISCUSSION QUESTIONS

1. Head writes that Korn's singer, Jonathan Davis, used a psychic to find out if he should audition for the band. Do you ever find yourself reading horoscopes or even tempted to visit psychics to "tell your future"? How do you think God feels about his people getting advice from psychics?

2. Head discusses how he could relate to the band's dark music because of the problems that he had with bullies and his parents growing up. Do you ever find that music can help you in that way? If so, how do you use music as your outlet?

3. Head became addicted to speed (methamphetamines) while he wrote music for the first Korn album—for him it was a temporary way to deal with the craziness of his new life, but it soon began ruining his life. What are other ways Head could have dealt with his life's difficulties? What role does Christ play in your attempts to get through hardship?

5. everything changes

At the end of those two weeks, Ball Tongue came to my apartment to get me out of bed for a while, and he took me over to this clothing company called Soul which was going to hook us up with some free clothes—one of the benefits of being in a rock band. When we walked in, I saw this cute little skater girl sitting at the front desk, answering phones.

Her name was Rebekah, and what I noticed first about her were her big, beautiful, blue eyes. Her hair was light brown cut into a bob, and she wore these baggy skater pants that made her look kind of wild. By the way she was smiling at me, I could tell she dug me, and before Ball Tongue and I left with our free clothes, she and I hung out and talked for a while.

For the next few days, I couldn't get this girl out of my mind. A couple weeks later, I saw her outside this club called 5902 where we played all the time, but since she wasn't twenty-one

Rebekah and I began to get serious right as Korn began to take off. This photo was taken pretty early on in our relationship when the whole limo thing was new to both of us.

yet, she couldn't get in. I decided to hang outside with her, and we kicked it for a while. I asked her if she wanted to go on the Korn Party Bus to a show we had in L.A. a few nights later. She agreed, and when that night came, we really hit it off.

We started hanging out every day, and I quickly fell in love with her. She was wild and kind of a spaz, so she rubbed most of my bandmates the wrong way, but she didn't care what anyone else thought about her, and neither did I. Looking back, I can see that she had me in the palm of her hand. I kept hanging out with Rebekah, and as our relationship grew, she eventually moved into my apartment with me.

At the beginning of our relationship, things were really great. But after a while, she started getting really weird—almost evil. She would attack me physically, like she was an animal, and she freaked out all the time, worrying about crazy stuff. The cute skater girl I had met at Soul disappeared, and I had no idea why.

It didn't take me long to figure it out. She had been hanging out at her girlfriend's house a lot, and they were doing speed over there. She was acting just like I had acted when I had been on my speed binge a couple of months earlier. I confronted her about it, and though she tried to deny it, I knew the truth. I kicked her out of the apartment. She was just too much trouble, and at that point I didn't want anything to do with anyone who did speed.

Once she was away from me, Rebekah really calmed down. I think kicking her out was a good thing that made her realize she had a problem. She chilled out on the drugs and started pursuing me, writing me all these letters, showing up at my house, and calling me a lot. I just couldn't resist her. When she was fun, I loved being with her. And I really did love her.

So Rebekah and I got together again, but we weren't as close as we were before. She still needed a place to live, but I didn't trust her enough to come crash in my apartment.

getting signed, getting pregnant

Within a few months, Larry was talking to Epic/Immortal, and he was so sure we'd have a deal soon that I quit my job because, along with that record deal, we would be getting a big fat advance check. Turns out I quit too early because we didn't have a deal just yet, and I ended up having to leave my apartment because I couldn't afford it. I spent the next two weeks sleeping on Ball Tongue's couch, just waiting for that deal to go through. When it finally did, I got the shock of a lifetime: about a year after we put the band together, Korn was finally signed to a record label.

My dream was coming true.

Then Rebekah dropped a bomb on me:

She was pregnant.

This second shock couldn't have come at a worse time. Though my longtime dream of getting a record deal had come true, it was bittersweet because I knew that having a record deal meant we would have to start touring a lot. What was I supposed to do with my pregnant girlfriend? I couldn't take her with me; it wouldn't have worked. And what about when the kid was born? What then?

I didn't see any other way around it, so I asked Rebekah if she wanted to get an abortion. While I was the one who first raised the idea of an abortion, I made sure she knew that the decision was totally up to her. Rebekah agreed, so we made the appointment for two weeks later.

A week after we made the appointment, I headed to Indigo Ranch, a recording studio in Malibu Hills to start work on Korn's first album (called *Korn*). The idea was that Rebekah and her friend would go to the appointment, Rebekah would get the abortion, and then she would come join me at Indigo Ranch. While I was waiting for her to show up, I did a lot of drinking in the studio. We had all quit doing drugs when we first went in, and since Ross was a big, obsessed health nut, he had us all drinking wheatgrass shooters every day. Within a couple weeks, though, we started falling back into our old habits.

I started using speed again, and so did Munky. Jonathan recorded most of his vocals on speed. It was really easy to fall back into it because Ball Tongue started using again, and he would drive up from Huntington Beach to drop it off to us. And of course, we were drinking the whole time.

Drinking and drugs aside, it was pretty cool to be in the studio, recording an album for a major label. Although I knew a lot about recording from my time at L.A. Recording Workshop, I didn't use any of it, and instead I just let Ross go nuts, since he seemed to have it under control. Besides, I had partying to do.

When Rebekah finally came up to the studio on the day of her appointment, she gave me yet another shock:

She was still pregnant.

She was unable to go through with the abortion; instead she decided to have the baby and put it up for adoption. I didn't know how to feel about her choice, but the truth was I didn't know how I felt about either abortion *or* adoption. In my mind, it was totally up to the woman. I even thought if you got an abortion early enough, it was no big deal. (I don't feel that way now, but I was very confused about a lot of things back then.)

At the time, Rebekah was still homeless, so I let her move back into the already crowded apartment I shared with my band. In the meantime, she got an adoption lawyer to find parents for our child.

new management

In addition, I was heavily focused on Korn. We had finished the record, and it was about to release. When Rebekah was about seven and a half months pregnant, Korn hit the road for a three-week tour with Biohazard and House of Pain. In the beginning, I loved touring and everything that came with it—the live shows, the fans, the parties, the adventure of life on the road. The first time I signed an autograph was on that tour.

But the reality was that I didn't have much fun because of all the other things going on. Don't get me wrong, I did what I could to enjoy myself, but my mind kept going back home to my girlfriend.

She was going to have a baby.

My baby.

For the first time there was something in my life way bigger than music or even a relationship—I see now that God was trying to wake me up. It was another sign; I just didn't notice it.

For months, I had avoided thinking about the adoption, and as a result, I still didn't have a clue how I felt about the whole thing, how I would react when the baby was born, or how I would deal with any feelings I might have. All I knew was that I really wanted to be in this band, but it wasn't as important to me as what I was dealing with. I wanted very much to be back home, but I couldn't. I had to stick out the tour. I'd come this far; how could I quit now? This was supposed to be my dream.

Toward the end of the tour, Larry resigned as our manager, and someone over at Epic recommended these two managers named Jeff and Pete. After we interviewed them a few times, they seemed to be a good fit for us, so we hired them. A few years later, Jeff and Pete would go on to create a hugely successful, mega-management firm, but back then they worked out of a little office in a rented house in L.A., with a few filing cabinets. As Korn grew throughout the next decade, so did they.

When the tour was finally over, our record released and we had a few weeks back home before we were scheduled to leave again to support our record. I was glad to be at home for

Rebekah, but I still didn't know how I felt about putting our baby up for adoption until I actually saw the baby face-to-face.

the miracle of life

Our baby girl was born at the beginning of 1995 early in the morning, and everything inside me instantly changed the moment it happened. At age twenty-four, I was a father. I felt a wave of intense love inside of me that I had never felt before in my life and didn't even know I was capable of feeling. I instantly thought to myself, *I can't give this baby away.* I remember it like it was yesterday. The hospital staff took the baby for some routine tests and procedures, and while she was gone, they started fixing Rebekah up.

With the baby and Rebekah occupied, I decided to take a walk by myself. Outside the hospital, I found a bench and sat down, all alone, and watched the sun come up, all the while feeling like my heart had been sucked out of my chest. Tears began to pour down my cheeks. How could I let this baby go?

I panicked. Something in me was screaming that I would regret this day for the rest of my life. It was so loud that I almost ran back inside and called off the whole adoption, but then I thought about the adoptive parents. They had been waiting for a child of their own for a long time *before* they met us. They had been with us almost the whole time during the pregnancy, going to the doctor's appointments, expecting their child. They were there at the hospital, early in the morning, waiting outside to meet the new addition to their family.

Though we still had full power to cancel the adoption, we only considered it for a little while. Rebekah and I didn't talk much in the recovery room, but it was clear that we both had the same question racing through our minds: *How can we give away our own baby?* In the end, we knew our child would be better off with those nice people. Rebekah wasn't ready for that responsibility, and I was going on tour in two weeks. It just wouldn't work out.

We gave that couple our first—and *their* first—child.

A couple of hours after the baby was born, one of the nurses brought her back in to us so we could have a few minutes alone to say good-bye to her. I took her in my arms, and all the emotions I hadn't felt while Rebekah was pregnant came pouring out of me like a flood. I cried and cried. A part of me died that day. For the few moments that I saw the baby, it was as if that empty space inside me had been filled. Even though I was becoming a rock star, there was nothing in my short career that felt so good. I couldn't believe I was giving away this little miracle of a child. I had signed her over to someone else to raise her. My heart couldn't take it. Before I knew it, our few minutes were up. The nurse came, took the baby, left the room, and that was it. The only way we'd ever see our baby again would be in photos.

We were both in total shock. While we had known this would be hard, I don't think either one of us was prepared for the emotional trauma of this decision. We were devastated.

Later that night, Rebekah was discharged from the hospital, and we immediately went to a friend's house and did a ton of speed together to help deal with the pain of giving up our baby. I was hurting like I never had before. With nothing solid, permanent, or trustworthy to lean on in our time of need, we reached out to what we could touch—and use.

We didn't talk much at all. We just sat there, high on meth trying to deal with our broken hearts in silence. We figured the meth was just a temporary fix; it was what we needed to kill the pain at the moment, but it was a sign of things to come.

We ended up staying up for a few days without any sleep. When we finally crashed, we slept for two days straight. I woke up to the sound of a huge motor running outside my apartment.

It was Korn's tour bus, waiting for me to get on board so we could go hit the road for almost the next year.

With the sound of the engine in my ears, I looked at Rebekah, who was still asleep next to me. I thought about how completely devastated her heart must've been after carrying the baby for nine months and then giving her away. If I hurt as much as I did about the whole thing, I couldn't even imagine what she felt inside.

I didn't know how I could leave her there all alone, but it was time to go tour. Time to leave my girlfriend at home all alone. Time to *really* start living my childhood dream. Time to become a rock star.

DISCUSSION QUESTIONS

1. Head figured out that his new girlfriend, Rebekah, was on speed during the early stages of their relationship. Do you think he should have broken it off with her right then? If so, what are some other important reasons to break off a relationship?

2. When Head found out that Rebekah was pregnant, he suggested she get an abortion. How do you feel about this? What do you think God's opinion is? (Back up your opinions with scripture.)

3. Rebekah decided to not go through with the abortion. We don't know her reasons, but perhaps someone encouraged her not to do it. If any of your friends were considering abortion, would you step in and get involved? If yes, describe how.

4. Rebekah and Head's baby girl went up for adoption instead. Do you know anyone who has adopted children

or has been adopted? If so, do you know how they feel about their adoption? In what ways can you share Head's story of adoption to encourage someone who's been adopted?

5. Rebekah and Head were heartbroken when they had to give their baby to the adoptive parents. If it was the best move for everybody, why do you think they were so upset?

6. blowups and meltdowns

As the bus pulled away from my house, I went straight to my bunk and fell asleep. I was still coming down off that speed binge, and the only times I woke up were to go to the bathroom. Other than that I slept the whole three-day trip from Huntington Beach to New Orleans. Or maybe it was a five-day trip. I don't know—I was asleep.

By the time we got to New Orleans, I had some of my strength back, so I decided to do something random. I let Fieldy shave my head into little squares. I then bleached the squares, which made my head look like a soccer ball. So, instead of calling me just plain Head, everyone started calling me Soccer Ball Head.

That first night on the tour, we opened for Bad Religion and did not go over all that well. We started playing, and the crowd just stared at us, like, "What are these guys doing playing with an old punk band?" They didn't know what to make of our sound

---

Soccer ball head. This is when I shaved my hair off just before the Sick of It All tour.

and style. After that show, we spent two weeks on the road with Sick of It All—another punk band that didn't really fit our vibe. The truth, of course, was that no one fit our vibe—we were so different from everything else out there.

At this point, touring was pretty much what I expected it to be. All the bands we had played with attracted a lot of crazy kids who just wanted to party—which was exactly what we wanted to do. As the tour went on, word about our show and sound started getting out, and crowds became more receptive to us. We were rocking it every night, and people were loving us.

Rebekah and I talked almost every day, and things were cool between us. We spoke about the adoption, telling each other that it was what we had to do and that the baby was better off, but we knew we were wrecked over it. I missed Rebekah a lot. After going through that intense childbirth experience with her and after feeling that deep love for the baby, I had become much more emotionally attached to Rebekah. It was a very traumatic event for us, and she was the only person I could talk to about it, since I didn't think anyone else would understand.

When the Sick of It All tour ended, Jeff and Pete landed us a tour with Danzig and Marilyn Manson, which ended up being a huge career move for us. The shows were great, and the fans were even better, but unfortunately, on that tour we all started drinking a lot more. In addition, cocaine became a big thing for some of us, myself included. While speed was considered dirty and gross, for some reason cocaine was okay. That was our thinking, anyway. It was just a part of the whole scene of that tour.

using (and abusing) again

Back in Huntington Beach, Rebekah began using meth again, and I was worried about her. She told me she wasn't doing it, but I knew better. I could tell by how crazy she was acting.

She flew out to see me a couple times and started attacking me physically again. One night on our tour bus, I grabbed her arm really hard and she slammed me in the nose with her fist. Blood went everywhere, and I jumped in my bunk so nobody in the band would notice. I didn't want to cause a big scene. Rebekah felt horrible and cried for about a day over that incident.

I had never been in a physically abusive relationship before; however, with speed there seemed to be a first time for everything. The violence didn't happen all the time, but it did happen. Mostly, Rebekah screamed and yelled at me, saying stuff like, "How could you let me give my baby away?" Deep down, she knew it was the right decision for the child, but unfortunately, the drugs were clouding her mind and making it hard for her to see the truth. Of course, I was a drunk who'd been messing with cocaine, so my mind was pretty cloudy too.

After the Manson tour ended, we began our next tour with Megadeth. We had the good slot, coming on right before Megadeth every night. A lot of the people in the crowd were older metalheads and hardcore Megadeth fans, and sometimes they just didn't understand our music and they would yell at us between songs. One night we played an outdoor show, and there was a little section of water between us and the crowd, like one of those moats around castles. While we were playing, Munky felt something fly by his head really fast, and he just thought it was some random weirdness. After the song was over, he turned around and saw a knife sticking out of his amp cabinet.

I guess when I was reading about being a rock star, this stuff was in the fine print.

When the Megadeth tour ended, we got some awesome news: we had landed a tour with my childhood hero and idol, Ozzy Osbourne, which was the coolest thing that had ever happened in my life. I mean, here was this guy that I'd grown up listening to, and now I was going to be opening for him. But better than that, it meant I got to watch him perform every night. Front row! For free!

It was awesome. I couldn't have been happier when I was on that tour—until Fieldy and Jonathan sat me down in the tour bus and said they had some bad news: Rebekah was cheating on me. I couldn't believe it and tried to deny it, but they knew specific details—the dude's name, all that sort of stuff. That news hurt me so much, and I started crying immediately. I had done some crazy things on the road, but I hadn't cheated on her. It just wasn't something I even wanted to do. Besides, Rebekah and I had made an agreement to stay away from speed and be faithful to each other.

When I called her, she denied she was cheating on me and had excuses for everything. And I decided to believe her. I wanted to drop it because I wanted us to move on. I wanted her story to be true, because I loved her. So we stayed together.

After the Ozzy tour ended, Rebekah and I got a tiny studio apartment in Redondo Beach that worked out great. We were both so sick of the drugs and sick of all the people we knew in Huntington—we just needed to leave and get away from the drama, making a promise to each other to stay off drugs. We had a new start in a new city; we weren't going to let things deteriorate again.

life's not so peachy

When the tour with Ozzy ended, we learned that Jonathan's longtime girlfriend was pregnant. Rebekah and I tried our hardest to be happy for them, but it just brought back a lot of pain, forcing us to recall a lot of the questions that we'd tried so hard to let go of. The answers all seemed really far away.

While I was living with Rebekah in Redondo, the Korn guys and I were in the process of writing our second album (*Life*

Is Peachy). Once we had written enough songs for the second record, we went back to Indigo Ranch to start tracking with Ross, just like we did for our first record. And, just like we did the first time around, we started doing speed again. Rebekah even came up and did it with us. It was only a matter of time before our drug use led Rebekah and me back to being physically abusive toward each other. It just wasn't a good scene.

As for the band, I didn't really like the direction we were going, artistically. Not on that album. We wrote and recorded it in about two or three months, so we didn't make it as good as we could have. Our plan was to get the album done quickly so we could get back out on the road as soon as possible, but the quality of the record suffered a bit because of how quickly we did it—not to mention the fact that we were messing around with speed and alcohol way too much.

The drinking and the drugs had just become a part of our routine, and it was hard to avoid them. Looking back on it now, I should have seen that things were going to be a problem, but it was so hard to break the cycle. I had nothing to guide me to a different place, and so I made one bad move after another and figured everything would work out.

One of the songs from that record was "A.D.I.D.A.S.," which stands for "All Day I Dream About Sex." I didn't even show up on the day Korn wrote that song. I called in sick because I was so tired from doing speed the night before. The video was a trip. All of us Korn guys got into a car accident and died, and then we were put in body bags and sent to the morgue. My dad got up early one morning to jog on the treadmill, turned on MTV, and saw the video; he told me afterward that it really disturbed him to see his son getting zipped up in a body bag.

By then, another one of the guys in the band was married and expecting a child. Again, Rebekah and I tried to be as happy for them as we could, but we still couldn't stop hurting inside for giving our child away. When we got our first pictures in the mail of the baby we put up for adoption, she was so beautiful and looked so happy and healthy—but it broke our hearts all over again to see those photographs.

There wasn't much time to dwell on those feelings. though, because shortly after we got the photos, Korn was off on tour again—this time to Europe, while our new record came out. (Even though we rushed *Life Is Peachy* a bit, it still entered the Billboard charts at number three, which was a surprise to all of us.) I was actually pretty excited about touring Europe. My childhood dream was finally taking me somewhere I had never been before.

I wouldn't need any drugs while I was over there, either. For the next few months, I just played shows and got drunk every night—living it up, European-style. Being away from Rebekah was still hard, but I used partying as a distraction and for the most part it worked.

I got over my excitement pretty quickly; as soon as I was overseas, Rebekah started pulling her disappearing acts again. I would call her at our apartment, and the phone would just ring and ring. One day I called up my manager Pete and sent him to check on Rebekah. After he knocked on the door and no one answered, he looked in the window and saw exactly what I was afraid of: two people lying in the bed. When he told me, I freaked out. I couldn't believe this was happening again. At least this time she couldn't deny it. Pete had seen it with his own eyes, and I knew I could trust him. I knew the truth.

I called and called and called, and finally, *finally*, Rebekah answered the phone. I told her what Pete had seen. Of course, Rebekah denied the whole thing, saying her friend and her friend's boyfriend were staying at our house.

I decided, once again, to believe her. Deep down inside I knew the truth, but I guess I was afraid to face it because I didn't want to get my heart broken again. I wanted someone I could love and who would love me. I wanted someone I could come home to after months of heavy touring. As I look back now, it's very clear that I was addicted to a lot of things that were bad for me, including this abusive relationship with Rebekah.

When I finally came home from that tour, I was really happy to see Rebekah. I hoped that somehow things would be different for us. But just as things started to turn around for Rebekah and me, the road called Korn out again. This time it was for Lollapalooza, the traveling summer festival tour where we would close out our tour for *Life Is Peachy*. Snoop Dogg and Tool were both in the lineup for that tour, so there were parties every night. The whole thing was pretty out of control, and it didn't do anything to help me clean up my life.

Snoop had a huge entourage of dudes with him, and almost every night they had crazy parties with all kinds of alcohol and food like fried chicken and macaroni and cheese in their dressing room. Their buses always wound up leaving before ours, so Fieldy, Munky, and I would eat their leftovers.

follow the leader

After Lollapalooza, we all went home and chilled for a while. It felt good to relax, but after a couple of months it was time for us to make our next album (*Follow the Leader*). This was our third record, and we knew going in that we had to step up our writing to get to the next level, so we approached it with a totally different mindset than we had with *Life Is Peachy*. We were going to take our time and make it as good as it could be.

Fortunately, the studio where we wrote that album was in Redondo Beach, so I had much less of a drive than the other guys, who were all coming from either Huntington Beach or L.A. While recording that album, we all worked incredibly hard to focus our attention and write good, quality songs. Sometimes we stayed in the studio for eight hours a day, completely sober, writing awesome stuff. I remember after Jonathan wrote the lyrics to "Got the Life" we all knew it would be a big single. It had this cool disco beat to it, and the lyrics seemed really cool at the time:

> God paged me
> You'll never see the light
> Who wants to see?
> God told me
> I've already got the life
> Oh, I see.

I had no idea until years later how wrong we were.

Still, we could tell that the song was going to be big, and it was. The music video for "Got the Life" was split into three segments. First, Jonathan gets pestered by a bunch of paparazzi, and he ends up smashing their cameras with a baseball bat. After that Reggie and I give our expensive car away to a bum (who was played by a rapper friend of ours named Tre from the Pharcyde), and finally Munky and David drive their car off a cliff, and it blows up. (I gotta admit—it was kind of fun to blow up a car in that video.)

The huge single from that album was called "Freak on a Leash," probably because the video was out of control. It was our highest-budget video because of all its visual effects and animation. The coolest thing about that video was that we wound up winning some MTV Video Music Awards and a couple of Grammys too.

When the songs had been written and it was time to record, our daytime sobriety came to an abrupt halt. We started recording in this north Hollywood studio, and while we were there, things turned pretty crazy as we spent thousands of dollars on alcohol.

That's when I picked up another bad habit—like I needed a new one. I started driving home drunk from the studio every night. At that point, I had a new car, and I figured the cops wouldn't pull me over because I looked like a classy citizen. Looking back, I'm so thankful I didn't hurt anyone else or myself. I could have easily been pulled over or caused an accident. It was a really bad decision.

Despite the partying, we still managed to create a record that we were really proud of. All the crazy stuff from the recording process couldn't distract us from the solid focus that we'd achieved while writing. It was a good thing too because we weren't the only people who were pleased with the record.

It was playing well to everyone who listened to it and a whole lot of people were about to buy it.

DISCUSSION QUESTIONS

1. Head's schedule of touring and recording made it really hard for Rebekah and him to console each other about giving their baby up for adoption. Head didn't talk to his friends in the band about it because he didn't think they'd understand. Do you think hiding this pain from his bandmates made it even harder?

2. After Head and Rebekah gave up their baby for adoption, twice they were faced with a Korn member's girlfriend or wife having a baby, and it broke their hearts all over again. Because God allows these moments to happen for a reason, what do you think those reasons were?

3. Head recalls the lyrics to a famous Korn tune, "Got the Life," from their mega-successful album, *Follow the Leader*—it's kind of about not needing God. Considering everything Head had gone through up to this point, how do you think God felt when Head played the song on stage?

7. jennea

Until *Follow the Leader* came out, most of my rock star life was pretty fun, but with big changes on the horizon, I knew it was always important to remember that this was my job, and I had to be responsible with the money I earned.

As far as money went, Korn was doing pretty well, so I decided this was the perfect time to buy my first house in Redondo Beach. It was a nice transition from apartment living. Rebekah and I lived there with her sister and her sister's daughter, and there was even enough space for a separate studio apartment under the garage that I rented out to a friend.

By that time, Rebekah and I had slipped up and done speed a few times, but on the whole, we were doing a lot better and had slowed down our using to the point where we only messed with it once in a great while. We weren't hooked, just dabbling, and that's how it went for a while. We settled into a nice routine,

Jennea, shortly after she was born. She brought the most amazing light into my life and it's been there ever since.

mostly happy with each other, while I was off writing and recording songs for our next album. Then I got another shock:

Rebekah was pregnant.

This time, we were determined to be parents, and we were so happy. We were older (I was twenty-seven years old) and more stable, but more importantly, we just knew we could make it work. We figured having our own baby would cement our relationship together forever.

Still, there was one hitch: I didn't really want to do the whole marriage thing because one of my worst fears in life was getting divorced and losing half my money. I mean, I loved Rebekah and all, but marriage was a big step. Besides—things were fine the way they were; why change them?

The problem, though, came down to money. Even though I was making decent money, I still wasn't rich. The first time Rebekah had been pregnant, the adoptive family had taken care of all the costs associated with the pregnancy—from doctors' bills to the hospital stay, they covered it all. Not surprisingly being a rock star didn't offer me health insurance at that time, and I didn't want to pay cash for all the pregnancy expenses, so I decided that I needed to get medical coverage for Rebekah. When I checked into it, I found out that insurance for Rebekah and the baby would cost a whole lot of money, but if we were married, it would be significantly cheaper.

So in a move that was probably one of my least romantic, I decided to go ahead and marry Rebekah in the name of more affordable health care. But I really did love her, so I felt good about it. Rebekah didn't want to have an actual wedding with a minister, bridesmaids, or other traditional roles, and instead we just looked through the Yellow Pages for someone to marry us. I have to admit, at the time, I liked the idea mainly because I wouldn't have to fork out thousands of dollars on a wedding.

We wound up getting married at a place in a strip mall that looked like one of those stores where you could rent mailboxes and ship packages. On the day we got married in March 1998, we cried some *happy* tears for the first time ever. We decided to put off our honeymoon until after she had the baby, so there we were, husband and wife, in a nice little house, with a baby on the way. Things were going to be great.

And they were great for a while, but I always managed to mess things up a few times along the way. Like when I talked Rebekah into calling one of her friends to score me some meth. I would make my pregnant wife go and score me speed while I waited at home because I didn't like her friends. This was definitely one of my trashier moves.

After she brought it home, I would get high and stay up all night messing with my guitar. Sometimes, the day after I did the speed, I would have those familiar fits of rage—at times I'd even hurt Rebekah. She would hit me, too, and we used to joke around and call the bruises that we gave each other love marks. They were anything but.

Somehow in between these episodes of mine, we managed to be pretty happy—a functioning dysfunctional couple. Though these episodes happened only a few times, I soon realized that my behavior toward my wife was totally unacceptable and I had to change fast.

So a couple of months before the baby was born, I decided to get completely sober and take a totally new approach to life. I just said no to all drugs and alcohol and firmly committed myself to getting clean. I even started eating right and working out. It felt unbelievable, and for the first time in years, I was clearheaded. I could focus on things in a new way, and I hadn't ever felt better.

jennea

Being clean made it so much easier to appreciate my daughter's birth in July. I can't even describe what life was like when my baby girl came into the world. The breath of life that happened when she entered the world was the most awesome thing. A complete miracle. We named her Jennea.

I was in tears. Rebekah was in tears. *Everyone* was in tears. I looked at Jennea as I held her in my arms. I was a father. I was a *father!* I couldn't believe it. It was as if some of the pain from giving up my first child was healed the second I laid eyes on her. Not that she replaced the love I felt for my first child, but I felt like I had been given a second chance to be a real father. Beyond that, it felt like Rebekah and I had a second chance at happiness together.

I was just sure that adding Jennea to our family was going to encourage both of us to make responsible choices for our lives. We were both going to do things differently. We were clean and sober and our future was lying there bundled up in our hands. This time, the baby was ours. *We* were the parents—no one else. And we were going to be the best parents we could be.

Fieldy and Jonathan already had kids themselves, and when they both came up to the hospital to congratulate us, I was so proud to show them my baby. Now that Rebekah and I had our own kid, I was positive that this would bring us closer to them and their families. Everything was going to be good from then on.

Starting with the day she was born, I held Jennea all the time, looking into her little face and thinking, *She is perfect, and I never want to leave her.*

But it turned out I didn't have a choice. A few weeks later, I had to go on tour in Japan. And as usual, that tour ended my brief and sober happiness.

sobriety ends

Leaving my family for that tour was incredibly painful. While I was really bummed that I had to go, at the same time I was excited to go to Japan for the first time. Our first show went really well too. In fact, it went so well that I decided to have a beer to celebrate. Just one, though.

After that, I decided to have a few more.

After that, I wasn't sober anymore. Just like that, I was back to my old ways, and things went on like that for the rest of the tour.

When we got back to the States, we did this huge press campaign to promote *Follow the Leader*, and shortly thereafter, with our managers, we all came up with the idea for a tour called "The Family Values Tour." The idea was to create a tour that we could put indoors with a bunch of crazy stage props for each band—like an indoor Lollapalooza.

We put a lot of other bands like Limp Bizkit and Ice Cube on that tour to open for us, and it worked. During that tour, we started selling around one hundred thousand or more copies of our album a *week*. We got huge. Fast. It was crazy. I was tripping; we *all* were tripping. We didn't know how to take it all in, how to deal with that success.

Sometimes we dealt with it by fighting. For once, Rebekah and I were fine, but in the band, things started to break down a bit. The pressure was intense—the eyes of everyone in the media and in the industry were on us, and it was almost too much to bear.

It was around then that Jonathan hit some very dark times, at least in part because he was the front man and felt the pressure the most. He started drinking a lot of Jack Daniels, which had a very negative effect on him and forced him into these phases where he'd just cry and cry, all night long. Jonathan had a bodyguard, Loc, who basically put him on suicide watch because Jonathan would talk incessantly about killing himself. In addition to his drinking, Jonathan was really struggling with anxiety, and so he saw a lot of doctors to try and treat this problem.

Unfortunately, none of them really helped, but one day he started taking Prozac, and he's been sober ever since. Seeing him calm down really helped the rest of us get over the anxiety of being famous, and when it came time to record album number four, we were all pretty well-adjusted to the fame.

where's the happiness?

We had achieved a level of fame that I never thought was possible. I'd always wanted to be a famous rock star, but this was so much bigger than I'd ever imagined. It was fun, but it wasn't what I'd dreamed it would be. I don't think that it was what any of us dreamed it would be. When I used to think about fame and the rock star life, I always pictured myself being extremely happy. I pictured myself having fun all the time and loving life. I never saw myself as an out-of-control alcoholic and drug addict. I never imagined one of my band members would become suicidal. I never thought the pressure would be so serious that everyone in the band would fight all the time.

And I certainly didn't think that I would have a wife and a daughter sitting at home without me, missing me for months at a time while I was missing them. I never thought about how hard it would be to leave them behind to go on tour. I had assumed that when you become famous, everything falls into place and is automatically perfect. Instead I reached another level of success and felt empty and alone—God was giving me yet another sign pointing the way to him, but I kept going on my own path.

Just about the only thing that went as I envisioned was the satisfaction of making music, the satisfaction of having fans who loved the music that we created and loved to see us play live. On some days that was enough to make it all worth it. But in the end, all of the other dramas involved were enough to kill that excitement for me.

By then, the Korn shows were getting even more out of hand. We were playing all these huge concerts because *Follow the Leader* had become so big. And because of that, the backstage partying was getting huge too. I wasn't comfortable bringing Rebekah and Jennea on the road with us—there was just too much partying going on—so I had to go it alone.

Everyone in Korn was married by then, and we had a rule within the band that wives could only stay out on the road for three days at a time. We would try to time our wives' visits to happen at the same time, telling them that it would be more fun if another wife was on the road with them. But really, we just wanted them to come and go so they wouldn't take up our party time.

With all of this partying, all this drinking, and all these drugs, it was supposed to be this big fun time. We were playing bigger shows than ever for thousands of fans who dug our sound and even had our songs memorized. This wasn't like the tours when we were starting out—now we were the headliners, and people were there because of *us*. Sometimes the bands that opened for us would get booed by our fans the same way we got booed by Megadeth fans.

Although all this big stuff was happening, I was starting to get a little depressed because deep down inside, all I really wanted was to be at home with my family. The way the cycle of my life played out, I could never be truly happy where I was. If I was on the road, I would think about being home. If I was home, I'd be focusing on making a new record. There was never a point were I could relax and be satisfied with life and with my family. When I wasn't with Rebekah and Jennea, there was this empti-ness inside of me, and the only time it went away was when we were on stage. Except for being on stage, I didn't like being on the road that much. Besides performing, everything else I could have easily given up.

Despite my sadness, I never let on to the rest of the band that I was unhappy; I always covered it up with heavy partying. I was always trying to make people laugh by acting funny and doing stupid stuff—all while being wasted. That's how I've always been, I guess—getting drunk and acting like a clown was really the only way I knew how to be.

After the Family Values tour ended, things calmed down some for us. Over the course of the tour, we'd adjusted to the idea of being famous and had overcome much of our anxiety surrounding our success; but there were still some divisions between members, and these emerged when we went into the studio to record our fourth album, *Issues*.

There were all these tensions that came to the surface while we were making that album. David was fighting with Jonathan and Fieldy, and the whole band had problems with Fieldy. He'd been my best friend for years, but even *I* was getting sick of him. With every album Fieldy's attitude seemed to get worse and worse. He loved hip-hop, so he was really trying to live this big rapper lifestyle—but it also was giving him a huge ego. By the time we got around to recording *Issues*, we were all making fun of Fieldy behind his back, calling him a wannabe rapper and stuff like that. Why behind his back? Because we were afraid to say something to his face. Fieldy was just brutal when he argued. He would go for the jugular and say the most hurtful things, just to win the argument. (For the record, I've heard Fieldy has worked out his issues and is a really cool guy nowadays.)

I guess we were all tired of each other, the way any group would be after years together. We were a hard-working band— touring, recording, doing interviews, and making videos. It was taking a toll on us. We had this joke, calling every day Groundhog Day; our lives were just like that Bill Murray movie when his character wakes up every day, and it's the same day over and over again. On the road, we woke up every day late in the afternoon, ate dinner, played the show, then partied until the wee hours of the morning. The next day we just repeated it. Through all this, the shows were the only things that remained exciting to me, and after the shows were over, the rest of the day was inevitably a drag.

back home

When I finally had some time to get away from the guys and head home before we started writing and recording *Issues*, it made me happy. Whenever I got home from a tour, I would be so excited and glad to be back, where things weren't always so crazy.

Jennea was still little, and I had a lot of confidence that our new young family was going to work out perfectly and that our problems would be a thing of the past. When we had our addictions under control, Rebekah and I *did* work out. We really were happy. We were both really goofy, so we made each other hysterical all the time, doing funny dances or making funny faces to try and make the other person laugh.

We had some good vacations too. When Jennea was four months old, I took her and Rebekah on tour to Australia for a week. It was awesome. We stayed at the Gold Coast and had a blast. Later on, we went to Hawaii together and did some scuba diving and snorkeling. We also took horseback-riding trips through the mountains to these beautiful waterfalls. We were happy and in love. But whenever it seemed like things were going well, they'd always get bad again, and every time they got bad, they'd be worse than ever.

A lot of the time, we put up a big front. My parents only lived a couple of hours away, and when we would visit them, we did our best to act like everything was okay—even though I'm sure my parents could sense something was wrong. Some of the time we really were happy, but most of the time we just acted happy in front of people and then fought a lot at home. Well, *when* I was home. Because more often than not, I was out on tour.

DISCUSSION QUESTIONS

1. After Rebekah got pregnant again, she and Head decided they wanted to be parents—it was a second chance for them, Head says. In what other ways does God give us second chances?

2. Sometimes couples believe that having a baby together will help their relationship; it's also been said that having a baby will make a good relationship better and a bad relationship worse. What's your opinion? Why?

3. When Korn got rich and famous, it seemed to raise tensions and hurt band relationships. You'd think that when you get so much handed to you, things would get easier, not harder. Why do you suppose so many rich and famous people run into so much personal turmoil?

4. Can you think of places in the Bible that talk about cures for Korn's disease of success?

8. the worst low

Being on the road all the time really did take its toll on my marriage. My absence made Rebekah resent me and my career—she had to stay home alone with Jennea while I was off partying and drinking. I would come home just beat up from all the drinking I did on the road and promise myself I wouldn't drink while I was back. But then I was so used to the alcohol that my body would crave it, so I would go through withdrawals and cave in. The drinking was really beginning to have a bad effect on me.

In addition, I was still battling with my anger issues that I had never properly dealt with. It was just like my relationship with Shannon. When I was away from Rebekah, I would think about how much I missed her and loved her, but when I was with her,

Amidst all the craziness, Rebekah, Jennea, and I took some pretty awesome vacations. This picture was taken at the Gold Coast during Korn's tour in Australia. I was nervous bringing Jennea this close to the tigers, but they were gentle.

she would get on my nerves. Little things that she would say or do set me off just like when I was a kid.

On top of that, Jennea would act strangely around me. When she was around two years old, I would come home and she would look at me weird, then go to Rebekah. Then after about an hour, she would finally come sit in my lap. She barely even knew me—it broke my heart.

And Korn never stopped touring—just touring and touring and touring. It was hard. I wanted to be home more for my family, but I just couldn't. Music was my dream, but it was also my career; it was how I supported my family. Rebekah would call me while I was on the road, just freaking out, asking when I was coming home or why she couldn't be there with me. The whole thing made me think about getting my own tour bus and taking her and Jennea out on the road with me full-time, but I was too cheap to actually go through with it.

Things started getting bad when Jennea was a toddler. I wouldn't hear from Rebekah for a little while, so I would call home: some days she'd be good, some days she'd be gone. I remember screaming on the answering machine, "Pick up the phone! Where are you?" She would be gone for days; I didn't know what she was doing, or where Jennea was. When I would finally get ahold of her after she'd been missing for a few days, she would say, "Oh, I didn't hear the phone," and stuff like that. There was always an excuse—just as there had been when she used drugs. I just knew she was taking drugs again, so I had to come up with another plan to rescue my family.

big bucks, big move

Around that time, Korn got the biggest check we had ever received—twenty-five million bucks. We all totally flipped out over that amount, and I decided to impress Rebekah with my share of the money and move us back to Huntington Beach. She just didn't seem happy, and I thought if I could get her out of Redondo, she'd get off drugs.

I told her, "What if I buy you a nice house right next to the horse stables? I'll buy you a horse, and a house with a pool. You'll be close to the beach and everything."

She got really excited about the idea, and we moved down there. I bought her a white house in this perfect little June Cleaver neighborhood. We were living the good life. I thought I could buy her happiness. So did she, actually.

But as much as I hoped that money would solve all of my problems, it wouldn't. I put my faith and trust in the idea that with enough money we could get through anything, that money would be all we needed to rely on. The sad truth I didn't know then was that money would never provide the solution. No matter how much I had.

Still, it was cool for a while—until we got bored one night, found an old friend, and started dibble-dabbling in drugs. We didn't go off the deep end, just a little bit of meth here and there. Sometimes we would even do speed when Jennea was there with us, but we always made an effort to make sure that she was asleep. We'd put her to bed, do some speed, try to sober up by the morning, and then be tired during the day. For whatever reason, we couldn't stay away from the drug for long.

Whenever I left for the road, we would both agree to not do speed while we were apart, but Rebekah couldn't keep that agreement like I could. Although she had done drugs most of her childhood, from about age fourteen on, I still felt responsible for her being hooked. A lot of the time, I was the one who brought the drugs into our home—I was the man of the house, and I should've been the best I could've been at being a dad and a husband. But I didn't have any self-control, so I left myself open for anything.

woodstock '99

Not long after Rebekah and I started doing speed again, Korn was booked for the biggest show of our career, a little thing called Woodstock '99. Rebekah and I left Jennea with my parents for the weekend and flew to the concert for some hard-core partying.

First stop: a private jet we rented with some guys in Limp Bizkit, Mack 10, Ice Cube, and all our crews. That flight was crazy. The plane had three sections: the first was the chill lounge where Jonathan and all the sober people were; the second was where all the rappers and crew were drinking and betting money at craps (I think Mack 10 took everyone's money on that flight); the third was for all the people who just wanted to drink and do drugs.

That's where Rebekah and I hung out.

Anyway, all of us in Korn were so nervous about playing. There were over two hundred thousand people attending that concert, not to mention the millions watching on satellite TV. It was crazy.

To add to our nerves, it seemed like it took forever for the show to start, and as show time approached, all I could think about was how hard my heart was beating. When the lights finally went out, we started the intro to our first song, "Blind."

In the intro, we each had our own part that built the song up to this crazy, heavy groove that no crowd could deny. David started with his ride symbol. The crowd roared so loudly, it pierced my ears. Then Munky jumped in with his part. The crowd got even louder. Fieldy's bass part came next. More roars. After that I started the opening riff to the instrumental hook of the song—the heavy groove. By that time, Jonathan screamed his opening line that never failed to put the crowd into a frenzy: "Arrrrrre yooooouuu *readddddyyyyyyyyyy*?!?!?!"

A sea of people jumped up and down at the same time, creating a wave that spread throughout the crowd. It was an awesome beginning to an amazing show. Afterward we all hugged each other.

And then came the after-party. Woodstock had rented out this hotel for all the bands, and there was a party on every floor. Rebekah and I took some ecstasy and did a bunch of cocaine that night. We stayed up all night and fought most of the time.

The next day, we partied more on the plane until we landed and got into a limo that was waiting for us. Still a little too high from the cocaine, we started drinking in the limo on the way home to level us out before we saw my parents and Jennea.

It was about five p.m., and we were pretty drunk when we got home, so Rebekah decided she should sober up by diving in the pool. And that's what she did. Shirt, pants, shoes, and everything. She walked right past my parents, said a quick hello, and then dove in. When she came up out of the water, she had a bump on her head from hitting the bottom of the pool. I was trying to talk to my parents without slurring, but that was pretty much impossible. They were definitely looking at us funny, but after a little while they left.

why is my life so messed up?

When my parents left, around eight p.m., we put Jennea to bed. The house got so quiet and we were so drunk and tired that it only made sense for us to go to bed. But we didn't. We started arguing about something stupid (I don't even remember what), and the argument quickly escalated into screaming. Rebekah got right into my face and wouldn't stop yelling. Then it got physical. She charged me pretty hard, so I lost control and punched her in the face. Blood started pouring out of her nose, down her face and neck.

I was shocked at what I had done. I felt horrible.

I thought that would stop the screaming, but she got even angrier, and it made the situation much worse. After seeing all the blood, I told her I was so sorry and that I wasn't gonna fight with her anymore. But she ended up beating me up for a while. I just lay on the floor with my face in the carpet taking punches from her.

Finally, after about twenty minutes, she collapsed on the floor and passed out. I remember sitting down next to her, shaking, and crying while my wife lay beside me all bloodied. That weekend was supposed to be the best time of my life, but it turned into one of the worst. It was definitely a gutter moment, me sitting there thinking, *Why is my life so messed up? I have everything I need in life to be happy.*

As I would later learn, nothing I could hold in my hands then would make me happy or fix my life—and I had a lot of that stuff. I still lacked one thing . . . but it was nothing I could see or touch.

At that point, things weren't looking too good for Rebekah and me, but there was one last moment of hope in our marriage. Rebekah ran into one of her old hard-core buddies who went by the name of Scottish. Scottish used to slam a lot of heroin back in the day, but now he had cleaned up and gotten married. He had made a huge turnaround, and when Rebekah ran into him, it really inspired her.

Because of that run-in, she was convinced that we could do the same thing. We got really excited talking and dreaming of our future together, of being totally clean for good. Rebekah talked to Scottish a few times on the phone, and he always injected a lot of positive energy and life into her.

Then one day, Rebekah got a call from Scottish's wife. He had relapsed. And overdosed.

And died.

Rebekah was crushed, and just like that, every ounce of hope she'd built up went down the toilet.

"i'm leaving you"

Shortly after Scottish's overdose, it was once again time for me to go on tour—this time with Metallica and Kid Rock, and that was when Rebekah's drug habit progressed from bad to worse.

While I was on that tour, I got a call from a friend about some crazy parties going on at my house. Noise. Skinhead dudes. Throwing, breaking stuff. I called my house, but Rebekah wouldn't answer, or someone else would answer, say she wasn't there, and then hang up on me. The worst part was that I didn't know where Jennea was. I was helpless. It was a nightmare.

I'd heard she was hanging out with one particular guy—a skinhead and second-strike felon. When I asked Rebekah about him, she would always say, "Yeah, he's an old friend from the old days. He's like my brother. I'm trying to help him out." Yes, it was true—he was an old friend from the old days, just like Scottish had been. But he wasn't clean, and I knew he wasn't just a friend either.

As usual I bought her excuses for awhile, but then I got a call from a friend who worked in a pawn shop. He told me some skinhead guy had gone in there trying to sell a solid gold necklace with a medallion that said "Korn" on it. I recognized that medallion—a record executive had a few made up and gave them as personal gifts to every guy in Korn. And now some skinhead was trying to get two hundred bucks for it in a pawn shop.

One night I called Rebekah and asked her what was going on. I expected her to give me the same excuses as always. Instead, she said the last thing I expected to hear:

"I'm leaving you."

I lost it. "What do you mean you're *leaving* me?"

"I'm leaving you!" she said, screaming. "I'm going to divorce you and take half your money!"

I was totally shocked. This couldn't be happening. My worst fear was coming true. I was determined not to let her go.

"I'm sorry, Rebekah," I said. "Look, we can work out whatever we need to work out. I'll get my own tour bus and take you and Jennea on tour with me wherever I go."

"No," she said. "I'm leaving you."

It was too late.

And I lost all control. That was one of the worst days of my life. I pleaded with her on the phone not to leave me, but it didn't do me any good. Her mind was made up. My whole world fell apart, and it drove me crazy. It drove me back to cocaine, actually. I didn't know how to cope, so I dealt with the pain and stress the only way I really knew how to: drugs.

I kept calling but no one would answer the phone. Finally someone picked up, but instead of Rebekah on the other end of the line, it was Jennea's babysitter. She told me that Rebekah had hired her to watch Jennea for a few days. Why? Because Rebekah had split for Oregon, where her mother lived (in a house we'd bought for her). Rebekah knew I was going to try to talk her out of leaving me so, instead of sticking around to listen, she took off.

Just a few hours after I talked to the babysitter, my mother-in-law called me from Oregon. She said Rebekah had just arrived, but that she'd brought a bunch of partying skinheads with her, and now they were terrorizing the place. There was fighting—bare-knuckle fighting—going on upstairs. There was blood on the carpet, kids doing drugs, all kinds of crazy stuff going on.

My mother-in-law said she felt like she was in a horror movie, so she frantically told me I had to go to Huntington, get Jennea, and take her out on the road with me. Apparently, Rebekah was going to be heading back to our house in Huntington Beach soon, and my mother-in-law was terrified for Jennea to be around all that skinhead madness. The drugs had turned Rebekah into a monster, and all these people she was hanging out with were making her worse.

After that phone call, I knew that her mother was absolutely right: I would have to take Jennea on the road with me full-time from there on out. I mean, if Rebekah was doing all that stuff in Oregon, then she had to be acting the same way at home.

Everything felt incredibly traumatizing. I was scared for Jennea, scared for myself. I was furious with Rebekah, but I had nowhere to put my anger and frustration. The only thing I could focus on was Jennea. Once I had that conversation with my mother-in-law, I became anxious to get home. While I was freaked out because Rebekah had left me and I was grieving her loss as though she had died, I had no time to grieve.

It was time for me to be a father, and I knew what I had to do.

As soon as I could, I flew home, picked up Jennea, hired a nanny, and went back out on the road with her. In just a couple of days, I had become a rock star single dad, but being around Jennea took away a lot of my pain about Rebekah. Of course, I didn't have much time to worry about myself—I was too worried about Jennea losing her mother to care about my own loss. All I focused on was making sure my baby was okay.

It was just the two of us now.

DISCUSSION QUESTIONS

1. At this point, Korn was one of the biggest bands in the world and the touring schedule was intense and long. What do you suppose kept Head on the road, especially with a wife and baby girl at home and after experiencing a lack of affection from his parents while growing up?

2. It's fairly common for people in their mid- to late-twenties (like Head) to struggle with anger that stems from events that happened to them during their childhood and teenage years and weren't dealt with. What can you do about those issues *now*, before they become harder struggles later on?

3. As his marriage was deteriorating, Head (and Rebekah) thought happiness could be bought with the tons of cash he was getting now that Korn was so huge. Have you ever been led to believe that if you had more money you would be happier? Why do you suppose so many rich and famous people are miserable?

4. By the end of this chapter, Rebekah leaves Head. In what ways have you been touched by divorce? How does your relationship with Christ help you in times of sadness, whether it's for yourself or for your friends or relatives whose parents have divorced?

9. i fall to pieces . . .

I surprised myself at how well I held it together for the rest of that tour. It was so painful to see Jennea and know that her mother was not there for her anymore. But while I missed Rebekah too, just looking at this beautiful, smiling, little girl every day was enough to make me feel better.

I wasn't the only one either. Everyone else loved her too. All the guys in the band and on the road crew would take turns hanging out with her—she was very popular. Even our big security guards would hang out with her and take her for stroller rides. She was a huge hit.

Despite all the insanity, I still hoped that Rebekah and I could work things out. I thought if she could just see me with Jennea, she would realize what she had done and come back for good. I couldn't admit that our relationship was over. During one of our

This was me at my worst. It was taken between songs at one of our shows, when my body was filled with meth, pills, beer, and peanut butter and jelly sandwiches. At that point I had almost no energy to go on with the concert—or life.

phone calls, she finally said that her skinhead "friend" was actually her boyfriend. I'd known the truth, but it still really hurt to hear her say it.

And then my pride kicked in: How can I let this guy take my wife away from me? How can I let this woman make me look like a peon in front of everyone? Don't they know who I am? I'm a rich and famous rock star! All I have to do is say the word, and I can have my revenge. But in the end, these fantasies didn't do anything to make me feel better, and they didn't bring Rebekah back to me.

While I was on tour with Jennea, Rebekah went back to Huntington Beach and stayed at our house again—along with her crazy, skinhead friends. I didn't want those guys in my house, so I called one of my Bako friends who happened to live in Huntington Beach, a guy I just called D. Since D was known in Bako for being one of the toughest guys in town, I asked him if he could go over to my house and kick everyone out. He agreed. Just to be fair, I called Rebekah and left a message, warning her that I was sending someone over to change the locks and that she'd better be gone.

Fortunately D only found the babysitter Rebekah had hired. She was having a good old time living in my house with her new boyfriend. He booted them out and got the locks changed.

When I periodically spoke to Rebekah, she would talk a lot about taking my money in the divorce, and at first I was scared that she could do it. In the end, I offered her a specific, one-time settlement, and she took it. She signed the papers, and we were officially divorced. It was over for real.

But there was one thing left to do: figure out who got custody of Jennea. We both wanted full custody, and Rebekah fought with me on the phone about that all the time. I really did want her to be able to hang out with Jennea, because I knew my daughter needed a mom as much as she needed a dad, but

Rebekah was acting like a monster. I didn't want Jennea any-where near her in that state. Eventually, we set a court date for our custody hearing that would take place six months later, and when Rebekah didn't show up, I got full custody.

I finished the tour and came home with Jennea. The band had planned a huge break after that tour, so I had some time to process all the craziness that had been going on in my life. While having the downtime should have been great, I became incredibly depressed just being in that house that I bought for Rebekah.

jennea scare

A couple of nights after I got home, I decided to put Jennea to bed early so I could get drunk by myself. When she went to sleep, I started in on the beer. I was also a heavy smoker at the time, but I never smoked inside the house, so I kept going in and out of the house to have a cigarette, hanging out in this lounge chair by the pool that I always sat in.

After I'd gotten good and wasted, and smoked my last ciga-rette, I wandered back into the house and passed out on the couch. A couple of hours later, I woke up and figured I should go check on Jennea, so I went into her room—and freaked.

She wasn't there.

I panicked. I started screaming her name at the top of my lungs and turning the place upside-down. I couldn't find her anywhere. Somehow, I wound up back at the couch where I had passed out, and I noticed that I had left the back door open, the door that led to the backyard. To the pool.

My mind immediately jumped to the worst possible scenario: Jennea had wandered into the pool, and I was going to find her out there, drowned. I mean, what were the odds? I couldn't find my baby anywhere in the house, the back door was open—it didn't take a genius to figure out she was outside somewhere.

When I started to walk outside, I was so afraid of what I was going to find, but as I approached the pool, my heart flooded with relief. Curled up in that lounge chair I always sat in was my little girl, fast asleep. I guess she had woken up in the middle of the night and wandered out there, figuring that's where she could find me.

I picked her up and held her for a long, long time. I was so thankful she was still alive. I vowed right then and there to clean myself up so I could be the dad she deserved. I should have seen this as yet another sign from God—another way he was trying to wake me up—but even the thought of my own daughter almost drowning couldn't keep me clean for very long.

back to bako

After a few months of trying to clean up and get out of my depression, I decided to move us back to Bakersfield. I felt it was the perfect place to start my life all over. With my parents and brother (and his family) there, it was a great opportunity for Jennea to be around her blood family more often. It would help both of us to feel like we were a part of something bigger, something that wasn't tied to the band, money, or drugs. As I was preparing for the move back to Bako, the big break from Korn was coming to a close, and we were getting ready to start writing our fifth album, *Untouchables*.

We decided for this album that we needed a change of scenery as a band, that we needed to get away from everything—our families and all—and concentrate on writing music. A couple of the guys were also going through divorces at that time, so it was good for all of us to get out of Dodge. (Eventually, we all ended up getting divorced, by the way. Just as we watched each other start our families, we watched each other lose them. Our rock 'n' roll lifestyle was just too crazy for most people to stick around us for long.)

We settled on Arizona as a destination and wound up renting these four huge houses in Scottsdale, moving in our equipment, and heading out there to get to work. It was a great idea, but it had just one problem: it turned into some of the most intense partying I'd ever seen Korn do. Fortunately for me, I was sober, and so was Jonathan. The other three band members—and our crew—were not. They went at it *hard*.

The four-house setup was convenient for our different lifestyles: Munky and I shared a house with the crew, and it had a demo studio. That's where we did most of the songwriting—it was usually the sober house. David had a house to himself, one of the major party houses; Jonathan also had a house with a studio, so I'd go over there at night to do some additional writing with him. Fieldy had the last house, and it was the craziest. He generally had wild parties every night.

After we wrote *Untouchables*, we headed to L.A. to record, and when the album was done, it was time to hit the road yet again. By that point, we were all pretty tired of each other's personalities, so we each got our own tour buses. Five tour buses, on the road together. We hardly made any money on that tour because of all the money we spent getting from show to show, but it was worth it—we simply couldn't live with each other anymore.

I wasn't on the road very long before I started falling into my same old tricks. I dove right back into partying during the *Untouchables* tour, and after the tour when I went home to Bakersfield, things go a lot worse. I met a new friend, a cool guy who had a lot in common with me, including a past addiction to meth. We wound up talking a lot about our past with speed, and over time we talked so much about it that we both started wanting it. Eventually we ended up getting some. I had sworn to myself that I would never do speed again after I saw how it wrecked Rebekah and ruined our family, but my addiction was much stronger than the promises I made to myself. Somehow, I convinced myself that I could keep it under control. I decided that it wouldn't hurt to do it once. After that, I decided that it wouldn't hurt to do it once in a while. Then I was hooked again. I turned into a speed junky. I was in the gutter and quickly falling to my personal rock bottom.

After all that stuff happened, I realized I had a choice to make: my music career or my daughter. I couldn't have both. And since they were both a huge part of my life, it didn't matter which one I picked. It was going to kill me to be without either of them. Speed became my escape, a way to avoid making the choice, a way to put it off a little longer.

a horrible mess

Rather than trying to get myself cleaned up and taking the responsibility for raising my daughter, I asked my parents to take care of Jennea while I went on tour and shoved more alcohol and drugs into my body.

My life was a big, horrible mess. My career was great, but my personal life had become nothing but bad news. One horrible thing after another kept happening, and I couldn't understand why. When I couldn't come up with an answer, I thought speed could help kill the pain.

My relationships with my friends were horrible, but it was really easy to blame it on other people instead of myself. I felt like I had to quit my band, and I couldn't. I was so depressed about the whole situation—I had all this money, all this fame, but I was really missing out on all the good stuff in life.

For years, making music and making money had been like a religion to me, but it was clearer now, more than ever, that they were failing me. They had been my focus, and I had been convinced that somehow they could solve any problem. I came to see that this wasn't the case, so I turned to drugs as hard as I could. Speed. Coke. Pills. Alcohol. Every day.

We had doctors coming to our shows all the time—one of them would bring us nitrous tanks, and we would inhale balloons all night; then he'd write us prescriptions for whatever pills we wanted. It made me feel like a kid in a candy store because I was so addicted. I remember a surgeon used to come to our shows with a lot of drugs. He'd tell us his coke and ecstasy was made from his pharmacist friend and that it was the best you could get. He would party with us until six a.m. and then complain that he had to go work in the emergency room at nine.

Crazy, crazy stuff, man.

I knew I had to shake the drugs, but I just couldn't. For one thing, I was too addicted—part of me didn't want to quit. For another, they were everywhere. No matter where I went, I would find them. If I was at home, I would run into some friends who were users. If I was on tour, I couldn't go anywhere without seeing a pile of coke. I had nowhere to run.

cursed

The first tour I did in the middle of this drug-soaked depression was Ozzfest, during a beautiful summer that I paid absolutely no attention to. Though we played with a ton of great bands that summer, I don't think I saw a single one of them—not even Ozzy. Instead, I just sat in the back room of my tour bus, alone, every night.

I had a security guard/friend named Joshua living in the front part of my bus, and he'd always try to get me to do fun things, but I never wanted to leave my room. Most everyone in the band and crew came to the bus to try to get me to hang out with them, but I always said I wanted to be alone. Sometimes I heard Ozzy performing those same songs I listened to when I was a kid, but I never went to watch him.

That enthusiasm from Korn's early days was gone. I just sat there in so much dark depression and asked myself deep questions. *How did I get here? Why can't I enjoy this life? Isn't being a rock star supposed to be fun? Why is my life such a nightmare? Why do bad things keep happening to me?* It felt like I was under a curse because all I had were these questions about my life, and no one—not my friends or my family—had the answers. I was stuck. And it didn't look like I was ever going to get out.

I needed something—or someone—to rescue me.

The drugs really started to get in the way of my guitar playing too. I looked terrible. I started thinking that it'd be a relief if I would OD in my tour bus or hotel room. When you first do speed, you feel bigger than you are. It makes you focus, really hard, so if your mind is set on something good, everything feels so much better than normal. But if you're thinking about negative things, the drug causes such darkness in your mind that everything seems much worse than it really is.

I loved that "good" feeling, but I became a slave to it. I wanted to quit so bad—I'd been promising myself for months that I'd quit after this tour or that tour or this month or that month, but I never could shake it. I was addicted physically *and* mentally. With the depression and disillusionment speed brought, I was convinced I may never be able to quit doing it—and if I quit the band, I'd never be a normal, happy person. And that's why I started thinking about death. It seemed like it might be a good escape. In my darkest moments it felt like the only way out and the easiest, since at that time I was convinced death meant I'd just turn into dust and sleep forever.

Those dark thoughts wouldn't last, though. I would eventually snap out of it, get my mind off me, and think about Jennea. I'd wonder how she felt when she thought about her mom and dad not being around like her schoolmates' parents. I'd think about how unloved and rejected she must've felt sometimes. But for some reason I kept on doing drugs to avoid facing my responsibilities as a father. I didn't miss one day using meth; I couldn't get out of bed without it. Whether I was on tour or at home with Jennea, I always had speed in my system.

In the beginning of 2003, Korn was getting ready for a world tour, and instead of being excited, my first priority was packing. I spent two days packing my stuff so I could get my drugs nice and hidden where no one could find them (in my suitcase inside containers of deodorant, or in my clothes, or in vitamin capsules). This tour went all over the world: China. Japan. Italy. The UK. Australia. We rolled through a country in Asia where the penalty for drug trafficking—even if you had a single joint in your suitcase—was death, and I didn't care. I was too depressed to be scared of dying. And besides, I didn't know how to get speed on the road in another country, so I had to make sure I had my stash with me.

While you'd think an addiction as bad as mine would be hard to hide, I did a really good job of keeping it from my bandmates. Of course, they knew something was wrong. They noticed how skinny I was getting, but they thought I was just on pills (which I was), and somehow that was okay.

Remember, speed is a dirty drug—not like pills you can get from a doctor. In Korn, taking pills was like eating lunch or smoking weed; it was something everyone did. Almost everyone was addicted to something (except Jonathan—unless you count Big Macs), but they weren't so addicted that they hid their drugs and toted them into other countries. That was just me. But those guys never stopped making attempts to get me to hang out with them. That whole time I was on drugs, they always showed concern for me.

I went home to Jennea, but I didn't stop using. I would spend a little time with her during the day, but at night, after she was asleep, I was off to my closet to snort some lines. Sometimes, Jennea would wake up in the middle of the night and see me at my computer or whatever, totally high on speed, and ask me why I was awake. She always looked worried and would sometimes cry, like she knew something was wrong with me. I would tell her that I had just woken up, and that I was going back to bed soon, but it didn't comfort her all that much. She was worried about her dad.

I started buying tons of meth from this drug dealer I hooked up with in Bako. He would come over to my house in the middle of the night while Jennea was sleeping, and he would bring his shotgun with him, because I was just one of many stops he had that night. We sort of became prison buddies—I was stuck in my addiction, and he was stuck dealing drugs to support his family.

And this whole time, I had my kid living with me—my precious, five-year-old daughter, who could only sit back and watch as her dad wasted away on drugs.

DISCUSSION QUESTIONS

1. Because of Rebekah's dangerous behavior, Head took his daughter, Jennea, away and eventually won full custody. Do you know any single parents? It's probably the hardest job in the world. Challenge: Brainstorm some ways right now that you can tangibly help and love a single parent.

2. Soon after Head came home with Jennea, he got drunk and then had a huge scare that he couldn't find her—he felt a rush of relief when he finally did. Are there ways God has been "yelling" for you to get your act together? How have you been responding?

3. Head talks about how he could tell that Jennea was worried about him just by how she looked at him. Have you ever been worried about your parents? How did you reach out to them to let them know you were there for them?

10. . . . and get put back together

Although I had done a good job of messing up almost every area of my life, the one way in which I was actually doing something right was money. In fact by 2004, I was close to being set for life. I was making a lot of cash, and I wasn't wasting it. Instead, I was back in the real estate business with this guy named Doug. He was a regular guy from Bakersfield who had a great family and was smart and in charge of his life.

He was also a church-going Christian and something of a goody-goody in a way that reminded me of my childhood friend Kevin. And just like Kevin, he was always happy and upbeat, always in a good mood. He was just an all-around positive person, unlike anyone else I knew at that time. Because of his attitude,

---

When I wasn't touring, I tried to be there for Jennea, and do more normal things with her, like here when we posed for pictures together. In the end though, the drugs and my lifestyle made forming a close bond with her really hard.

I was really drawn to him, but I had no idea how important he would become.

Unlike Kevin, Doug never talked about Jesus or God with me. Our relationship was strictly business—the only way I knew that he was Christian was because someone else told me. Working together, we had a good time making real estate deals in Bako, and when we made those deals, we used Doug's broker, a guy named Eric, who also happened to be a Christian and also had his life together.

I really liked hanging out with these guys, mostly because they were just so positive, not to mention the fact that they were good businessmen. I trusted the decisions they made, and I felt like I could make a lot of cash in real estate by working with them. When I was thinking more positively, that became the goal that I carried in the back of my mind: get clean, get up enough nerve to quit Korn, then do real estate for the rest of my life.

a moment of clarity

Since I toured so much with Korn, I often had to do my real estate business while I was on the road. One day I was on tour and I called Eric to talk about some business. I wound up getting into a conversation with him about my life and how hard it was finding a balance between the band and my daughter. I told him how I was considering quitting the band, and he said something that really got me to thinking:

"You know, Brian, no one ever says on their deathbed that they wished they would've worked more. They always wish they had spent more time with their family."

And it hit me right then.

It was suddenly clear: I thought about Jennea, and how if I quit the band to be with her, I would have no regrets. If I stayed in the band, however, there would be all kinds of regrets. The problem was that I didn't have the guts to quit Korn. It was a big step for me. We were at the height of our career. Professionally, things couldn't have been better. We were selling tons of records, playing these huge shows, going all over the place, and every time I would start thinking about quitting, the drugs would get in the way. They just kept fueling my selfishness. I couldn't think straight about the whole thing, let alone make a decision. One day I wanted to quit the band, the next day I wanted to stay.

can't kick the habit

Then I devised a plan: kick the drugs for now, most likely quit the band, raise my kid, and then when she was all grown up, I could go back to drugs later in life. I found this clinic in L.A. that specialized in helping actors and musicians get clean, this really incognito place that kept everything quiet. I left Jennea with my parents, checked myself into a hotel, and took the meds the clinic gave me. I tried to sleep, but I couldn't—all I could do was lie there, depressed. The depression got worse and worse, and I started feeling like I'd go insane if I didn't do a line right then. The meds were powerless against speed. I went home and dove into my stash. In that instant, I gave up on quitting; it wasn't going to work this time. I really made an attempt to quit, and when I failed, it was very scary to me because it confirmed my worst fear: I couldn't escape meth.

In the meantime, we hit the studio to make album number six, *Take a Look in the Mirror*. Though it felt good to start working with the band again, the recording process did little to curb my addictions.

I don't have a whole lot of memories of that time because I used speed during the whole period we recorded and toured for that album. When we hit the road, I just did the same stuff.

Toured with Korn on dope. Went home on dope. I wasn't doing anything with anyone. I refused interviews. I even started to hate playing live. I'd had enough of everybody and everything.

In the middle of 2004, it looked like Korn was headed for a breakup, or at least losing a member or two. Jonathan and Fieldy had girlfriends who came on tour with us and started fighting a lot with each other; then Jonathan and Fieldy started fighting to the point where Jonathan wanted to kick Fieldy out of the band. I was disgusted, so I asked my tour manager to get me a ticket home, but he wouldn't do it.

I was stuck. Just like with drugs, I couldn't bring myself to quit Korn; I wanted someone or something *else* to make the decision for me, to take me out. I was addicted to the band, and I was addicted to drugs. Both of them were sucking the life out of me, and I knew I had to quit them both. But I couldn't. Jonathan and Fieldy wound up working it out, and we made it through the tour without canceling it.

I had my moments of temper too, just like the rest of Korn. I was playing poorly, so I started taking it out on my guitar tech during our shows. One time I got so angry about my horrible playing that I took my guitar off and threw it at my tech. He ducked, and it flew backstage where a bunch of people were walking by; luckily I didn't hit anyone.

I was just saturated with evil and depression. I was doing more speed than you can imagine. I had hit rock bottom. I was in the gutter

And I was dragging my beautiful five-year-old daughter down with me.

a cover i'll never forget

One day in between tours, I was sitting at home listening to Jennea sing. I was thinking about how amazing she was, how she was the cutest person in the world, and how hard it would be to leave her to go back on tour that fall.

Then I heard what she was singing.

It was the Korn song "A.D.I.D.A.S." (it stands for "All Day I Dream About Sex.") These words were coming out of my five-year-old little girl's mouth, and I knew right then that something had to change. I was already in the gutter, but that really made me feel like a piece of trash.

I knew it was time for me to try to reach out for help, so I reached out to Doug and Eric a little bit. Because of our real estate dealings, I e-mailed with those guys a lot, and in some of the e-mails I started to hint at how unhappy I was—not just with the band, but with life itself.

One morning I got an e-mail out of the blue from Eric:

Brian:

Not to get weird on you or anything, but I was reading my Bible this morning and you came to mind when I read this verse:

"Come to me, all who are weary and burdened and I will give you rest. Take my yoke upon you and learn from me, for I am gentle and humble in heart, there you will find rest for your souls. For my yoke is easy and my burden is light." (Matthew 11:28–30)

I don't know why but I had a very strong feeling this would mean something to you and that I should jump on e-mail and send it to you. Please don't take that wrong.

All the best!

Eric

I read his e-mail, and when I replied to him, everything came pouring out of me. I hadn't thought about my friendship with Kevin in a long time, but I told Eric everything.

"I'm a lost soul, man. My life isn't fun anymore. I asked Jesus into my heart when I was a kid, and I felt something inside of me. I want to get back to that feeling, but I haven't prayed or any-thing. I feel guilty for not ever going to church. Do you have any advice on where to go from here?"

Eric wrote me back within a couple of hours. He had some advice:

Brian:

Awesome message. I want you to get one concept . . . going to church does not make you a Christian any more than sitting in a garage makes you a car. A relationship with Jesus is personal. He is your confidant and friend, you can turn to him ANYTIME. He is ALWAYS accepting and no matter what you have done, he can release you from any guilt, pain, or shame you have. People in far worse circumstances have turned their lives around and come to know the unconditional love of God! You don't have to make a public spectacle of yourself to accept Christ into your life—you simply need to kneel down right where you are and say, "God, I'm sorry for my sins, please forgive me and come and live within me. Help me walk in your light, read your word daily, and rely on you for all my decisions. Let me be an example of you and let others see the change in me because I have made the decision today to give my life to you."

That's it. Then pray as much as you can and read your Bible every day and make good decisions. Your family will see a change in you, your daughter will see you in a different light, and you will have a peace that surpasses your understanding. I would love to come and sit with you to talk more about it.

Eric

jesus—my last hope

This message from Eric was really inspiring, and after reading it, I was almost ready to try Jesus out again, like I had when I was a kid. I couldn't help but think that I had gotten involved with Doug and Eric for a reason, and that just like with Kevin way back when, there was something else going on. The more I thought about Jesus, the more I needed him to be real. I needed him to help me with my life, to give me the answers that I couldn't get from anywhere else. He was the only hope I had left.

I couldn't shake the thoughts: *Is this why my life was so screwed up, because I hadn't done anything with Jesus since that day in my basement bathroom as a kid? Was Jesus calling me back to him so I could start my life over—his way? Would all the addiction, guilt, shame, and pain go away if I gave him my life? Was he giving me the positive thoughts in my mind? Was he the one telling me to leave the band so I could live for him? Could this stuff about Jesus be true?*

I had so much hope, but it quickly faded away when I thought about being a Christian. *You don't want to turn into one of those geeky people you see on the Christian channel on TV*, I thought. *Everyone would laugh at you. Don't be an idiot.* I was also concerned that Doug and Eric would start turning into weird Christians and start bugging me about going to church with them. It just wasn't something that I felt ready for. But then I had other thoughts that went the other direction. *What, are you going to stay in Korn, stay hooked on drugs, and die? You going to leave your kid fatherless?*

There was a battle in my brain—in my soul—and I wasn't sure who I was going to let win. This wasn't the drugs talking to me; this was something different. It was almost like—well, it sounds weird—but it was almost like God and the devil were fighting over my soul. Like it was a spiritual battle for my life, but it was up to me to make the final choice.

I had a lot of thinking to do.

inescapable signs

Toward the end of 2004, all sorts of weird stuff started happening to me. I ran into the guy who I had done speed with after the *Untouchables* tour, and after talking for a while, I found out he was now totally clean and living for Christ too. He invited me to go to church with him, but I didn't go.

Then I ran into an old friend named Bill who I'd known when I was a teenager. Back then, Bill was a wild punk rocker who used to go to all the same parties I did and always seemed to get into fights. But now things were different. He too had become a Christian, and he started telling me about God. The whole thing just felt too weird, though, and I freaked out on him, calling him a Bible banger, and told him to leave me alone.

In addition to these run-ins, one of my neighbors, a mother whose daughter was friends with Jennea, started to ask me if I wanted to go to church with her family. I never took them up on the offer, but it seemed to fit the pattern that had been developing. The whole thing was so unexpected. Where was all this coming from? Why, all of a sudden, were all these people trying to talk about Jesus with me?

Then there was my own daughter. My aunt Deia and uncle Tim had started taking Jennea to their church every now and then, and as a result, Jennea had started to ask me questions about God and Jesus. Questions I didn't have the answers for. When she would ask, I would just point to the sky and tell her that God was too big and far away for anyone to understand anything about him. I felt stupid for not being able to give her a better answer, and I got angry with myself for not knowing more about how to respond.

Everywhere I went, I ran into someone who wanted to bring up Jesus—this time the signs were becoming inescapable. And the whole time, I was still thinking about the final choice I had to make, but all that thinking still did not bring me any closer to a decision.

my vision of heaven

By November 2004, I wasn't quite done thinking yet, so I grabbed my drugs and hit the road for what would end up being my last tour with Korn. I spent that tour doing drugs and avoiding phone calls from Doug and Eric, since I was becoming increasingly worried that they were going to bug me about becoming a Christian after I had responded to Eric's e-mail. During that tour, meth made it a lot easier for me to ignore the voice in my head that was considering Jesus. Instead of the positive messages I'd been thinking about when I talked to people about Jesus, my addictions placed other messages in my mind. Instead of thinking about how good the future could be, I started thinking about suicide.

A couple of times during that tour, we had to fly to the next show because our buses couldn't make the long drive in time for us to play. Something very strange happened to me while I was on one of those flights. As the plane took off, I had a sort of a half-awake/half-asleep trance. A vision. It was way more than a dream. It was very vivid, like it was really happening. I'd never experienced anything like that before in my life.

In my vision, I was on a different plane, and I was fully awake. It was like a full-on movie in front of my eyes. We were taking off, just like normal, when the plane shifted crazily. I stayed totally calm.

Then the plane shifted again. It tilted.

The plane was going down.

I knew I was going to die.

I heard a huge explosion and then saw a big cloud of orange fire coming toward me in slow motion. As soon as it reached me, everything went white. I had been changed in the blink of an eye. No pain.

I was still in motion, moving upward somewhere, and I felt this heavy, heavy peace, like nothing I had ever felt before in my life. I didn't feel the burn or the explosion or anything. I just heard it, and then I knew what was going on.

I felt free. I had died and was going to heaven.

Then I woke up and screamed, "Whoa!" I shook myself, and everyone on the plane turned around to look at me. I thought I'd just been given a premonition of how I was going to die, so I started tripping. I didn't know if that plane was going down or what, but that vision was so lifelike that I was pretty convinced I was going to die soon in a plane crash. The plane landed fine, and I started to think about how I'd been doing a lot of drugs, so I wrote that vision off as a weird dream brought on by my drugs.

Something was in the back of my mind, though. I had convinced myself while I was on drugs that whenever I died, I would just turn to dust and sleep forever. But in that vision, I didn't die. I had been charred by the explosion, and I *still* wasn't dead. Instead, I started rising up toward heaven.

Was this another sign? What if I had been all wrong about what happens when you die? Was Jesus trying to reach out to me through this vision? Was he trying to tell me something? Was he showing me that I *wouldn't* turn to dust and sleep forever if I died, because there was life after death? Or was he trying to tell me that I needed to die to my way of living so I could be free and have peace in my life? Was he showing me that he was real?

And if that was the case, what did that mean for *me*?

I would soon get all the answers to those questions, but for the time being, I just tried to forget about the vision. At the time, it was too much for me to comprehend.

happy birthday, jesus

That tour ended a couple weeks before Christmas, and just after I got home, Eric showed up at my house with an early Christmas gift: a Bible, with my name inscribed on the cover. I was expecting the big Christian sales pitch, but he wasn't pushy at all. He just said, "Brian, if you ever want to talk to me about the Lord, let me know." And then he left.

That surprised me. I was sure he would be a pushy Christian now, but he totally wasn't. Even so, I put that Bible away and got back to my drugs. I did poke my nose in it a couple times— I felt kind of drawn to it—but I didn't really understand it, so I would put it back down right away.

Christmas came and went, and I was high the whole time. I felt pretty bad about it, though, because I knew Christmas was supposed to be about the Lord's birthday. I bought Jennea's gifts at the last minute on Christmas Eve and wrapped them all night until six a.m., all geeked out of my mind on speed. I think I re-wrapped some of them about five times to get them all perfect.

I woke Jennea up a few minutes after I wrapped them, and I watched her open her gifts. Then my parents, my brother, and my brother's family came over, but I was so wrecked from staying up all night that I didn't want to be around them. In the end, I told everyone I was sick and just lay in my bed to get away from them.

A day or two after Christmas, Jennea and I were at the grocery store. I was by the cake section when she came up to me holding a cake. She said with her sweet voice, "Daddy, we forgot to sing 'Happy Birthday' to Jesus. Can we buy him this cake?" I already felt guilty for doing speed on Christmas, not to mention the fact that then, at that moment, I was also on speed. Hearing Jennea say that freaked me out and still does. The Lord was calling me, big time.

I couldn't resist her pretty eyes, so I told her we could get the cake. We went home, and I put it in the pantry and forgot about it until the next night. Jennea was asleep, and I went to the pantry to get a snack. I saw the cake, and felt that same conviction again, so I picked up the cake and said, "Happy belated birthday, Jesus." And then I ate it.

A few days later, I was up at about five in the morning doing drugs when I got this enormous pain in my chest. It was like a vice grip. I couldn't breathe. I was sweating bullets. Convinced that I was having a heart attack, I staggered to my computer and checked out the symptoms on the Internet. I found a site that listed them, and I had every single one of them, so I called a friend to take me to the hospital. When I got there, the doctors ran a bunch of tests; it turned out I wasn't having a heart attack—but there were all these weird movements on my EKG they couldn't explain. They sent me to a heart specialist who ran all sorts of tests, put me on a treadmill and hooked me up to a lot of wires and crazy instruments to measure my heart. It turned out that my heart was actually okay, but I needed to quit meth very soon or my heart might not be able to take it anymore.

That scare was a push in the right direction for me, so when I got home, I called Eric and asked him if he would meet me at a coffee shop the next morning to talk. He agreed, and we set the time.

And then I did a bunch of speed and stayed up all night long—I was completely out of control.

DISCUSSION QUESTIONS

1. Head got reacquainted with God through his relationships with two guys from his hometown that he went into business with. These two guys didn't go out of their way to share their faith—they just lived it . . . and Head noticed. Do you think that's a good approach to evangelism? Why or why not?

2. Head was intrigued by Christianity, but he was also well aware of hypocritical and phony Christians out there—especially some of the ones you see on TV. How does this make you feel as a believer?

3. While Head was still considering Christianity, his Christian friend Eric gave him a Bible for Christmas—but no "Christian sales pitch." Was this the right approach? Should you keep pressing or back off after you've shared the gospel with a friend?

part two

god finds me

11. talking to god

When I met Eric at the coffee shop, I was still pretty tweaked out, but we sat down in a quiet part of the shop, and Eric started telling me about how Jesus loved me for no reason other than to love me. That it didn't matter what I had done up to that point in my life—Jesus still loved me.

When Eric was done, he suggested that I pray with him to ask Jesus back into my life. I thought, *No way. I've been up all night on speed, and I'm still high right now. If I pray this prayer while I'm high, I'll go to hell for sure.* I figured I had to clean myself up and get off drugs before I could even think about talking to God. Eric led me in the prayer, and I said it anyway, even though I felt a little bit pressured.

As I drove home, I started freaking out. I felt like God was going to strike me down or something for praying to him while I was high. When I got home, I went straight to my bedroom, found the Bible Eric had given me, and started talking to God.

Once I started to walk with the Lord, there was no stopping me.

"God, I didn't mean that prayer that Eric pressured me to say! I'm still on drugs, and I know I'm going to do more. Like, today."

I was true to my word too. I did more drugs that day. And the next.

And the next.

A couple of days after I met Eric in that coffee shop, I talked to Doug, and he invited me to go to church with his family that Sunday. I hesitated. I didn't know what to do; I didn't really want to go because I was still on drugs, but something inside me told me I should. So I agreed.

at church . . . and wasted

Saturday night rolled around, and I was still a slave to my routine. I put Jennea to bed and started snorting my lines. Stayed up all night. The next morning I was still really geeked when Doug, his wife, Sandy, and their two boys came to pick us up, so I threw on a hooded sweatshirt to try to hide it. We got to church and headed into the auditorium to go to the service. They had a band there and when the band started playing, all these people around me started raising their hands in the air. Some of them were crying. Some of them started yelling in other people's ears (I found out later that this was how they prayed for each other).

It was all too strange for me and it just freaked me out. These people were weirder than I was—and I had been awake for three straight days. But something inside me didn't want to leave. I felt a strong sense of love and peace. I stayed through the music, and then the preacher got up and started talking about God. They had these huge projection screens on either side of the stage, and there was a scripture up there that he was talking about.

It was Matthew 11:28–30. The same scripture Eric had e-mailed me a few weeks earlier. I just knew they were screwing with my head now. There was no way that this could be a coincidence. Eric must have told the preacher to put that scripture up there. Doug must've told him that I was coming, and so they had set me up. (It wasn't Eric by the way; it was God. That scripture was one way that God called me to him. I started seeing that scripture all over the place for the next couple of weeks.)

Then the pastor said something that really shocked me: "All you have to do is spend time with God and talk with him and all the burdens you have, all the heavy stuff you're carrying, will fall away from you."

Well, that got me really excited inside, because to me, that meant that I could go home, snort lines, talk to God, and then he would take away my addiction. That sounded like it was exactly what I needed, so at the end of the service, when the preacher asked if anyone wanted to ask Jesus into their life, I raised my hand and decided on my own to go through with it.

a brand-new life

Although I had told God I didn't mean that prayer I said in that coffee shop, this time, I meant it. January 9, 2005, was the day I began my new relationship with Jesus Christ. My life was never going to be the same.

It's worth mentioning that because meth is such an addictive drug, the success rate of kicking it permanently is very low. When you try to live without it, the depression that the drug gives you tells you that you can't—that you must have it to survive. But I knew I *had* to stop listening to the drug and at least give this God, this Jesus, a chance.

Immediately after church, after raising my hand to accept Christ in my life for real this time, I went home, put on a movie for Jennea, and went into my master closet, opened the safe, and grabbed the best bag of meth I had in there. I snorted a line, then sat there on the floor, a rolled-up bill in my right hand, and prayed.

"Jesus, that guy at church said you're real. He said all I have to do is hang out with you and talk to you and that you would take these drugs away from me. Search my heart right now. You know I want to stop. I want to be a good father for Jennea. I tried rehabs and they didn't work, so please take the urge to do drugs away from me. Forever. They've messed up my life. Please make me not want to die anymore, God. I don't want to leave Jennea without a dad. She needs me."

Then I snorted another line.

A couple of minutes later, the phone rang, but I let the machine pick it up. It turned out to be an old friend that I had done speed with a few times in the past. He was yet another person from my past who had become a Christian recently, and he was also a member of the church I had gone to that morning. He heard that I had been there and had raised my hand to ask Jesus into my life, so he was calling to encourage me in my new relationship with Christ.

I tripped out.

I'd just finished asking God to help me, and here was this guy on my phone two minutes later. A guy I could trust. I knew that God was telling me to admit my problem to this guy, but I fought it. I didn't want to talk to him—he reminded me too much of speed because I used to do it with him. Besides, I hadn't told any of my friends that I was so hooked on speed. Still, I knew I had to tell *someone* about my addiction, someone who could help me get over it. I was so ashamed. I had hidden this thing from everyone in my life for almost two years; I needed someone I could trust.

flushing my drugs

About a week later, I bit the bullet and called my old friend D. I told D that I needed to talk. One day, while Jennea was at school, he came over to my house and I told him about my problem. I took him into my bedroom, unloaded all the meth I had in my safe, and I asked him to throw it all away for me.

When he saw how much was there, his face dropped in disbelief. He almost started crying, he felt so sorry for me. He had never seen such a huge amount of drugs before in his life. He looked at me and said, softly, "What are you doing to yourself, man?"

I didn't have an answer.

Meth stinks, by the way. It smells bad. Especially if you have a lot of it. D was gagging from the smell as he emptied out all of my speed—baggie after baggie getting flushed down the toilet. But he carried on, and soon it was all gone.

I was nervous. I hadn't been able to kick it before. What made me think I could do it now? Somehow, I knew. This was the first time in two years that I felt like I could really quit. And not just speed—I chucked all my drugs, all my Xanax, Vicodin, Valium, Celexa. And my beer too. Beer—the one thing I never gave up for almost twenty years (except for that couple of months after Jennea was born). I gave it up that day.

The thing that tripped me out the most was I didn't have those depressing thoughts like I did before. God was really doing something awesome inside of me. I could feel it. It was time for the next step, so I called my parents and asked them to come over to my house to watch Jennea.

coming clean

I told them I had to go to L.A. for a week for some Korn meetings, but I was really going to check into a hotel in Bako, so I could sleep through my drug withdrawals. I got into my hotel room and got ready to stay there until I was clean. That was where I really learned to rely on God.

For the next two days, I only did three things: I ate, I slept, and I prayed. In that hotel room, I was alone with God, and I don't know how he did it, but he got me through those withdrawals fast. On one of those days, I woke up from sleep and started crying tears of hope. I thought I heard God tell me that I was his now, that he was going to use me and my music for his purposes from then on. But by the next day, I had written it off as my imagination.

Still though, I was listening to him instead of the drug, and two days later, I was ready to end my seclusion. It was nothing short of a miracle. Usually when someone quits speed, they sleep for two to four weeks straight and the whole time they struggle with these awful feelings of withdrawal, but there I was ready to start my new life after only a couple days. I began to feel like a positive person, and I wanted to be around people again. I left the room and started walking around downtown Bakersfield, which I had never wanted to do before. It felt so good to be outside in the sunlight.

In that single moment, my drug addiction began to fall away from me. I started talking to God nonstop. All I could think about was him, and all I could do was reach out to him with my heart. I figured that since I had ignored him for so long I'd better catch up and make up for lost time.

I went back to that church a couple of times after that first week, and I felt like a new man. I was feeling God touch me inside every day. I would just cry and cry for no other reason than because I just felt loved. I wasn't sad at all. I felt total peace. I had done drugs every day for almost two years, and now here I was, clean for a couple of weeks. I couldn't believe it.

I wasn't the only one who was tripping on it either. D also saw the transformation in me and he could hardly believe his eyes. While he wasn't a Christian, he could definitely tell that something had changed. I talked D into going to a church service with me one night that week, and he agreed.

When we were there, I prayed hard for God to reveal himself to D like he had done to me, and after the service, I told D what I had prayed for. I told him to watch for signs from God, because I believed that God would reveal his presence to him—just as he had for me. Signs were what had led me to him, and if he'd done it for me, I was sure that he would do it for D too.

D and I said goodbye and left, but a couple of minutes later, D called me, freaking out. When he had gotten in his car, he turned the radio on, and it happened to be playing the chorus of "Head Like a Hole" by Nine Inch Nails.

"I'm tripping out right now," he said. "Because when I turned on the radio, I heard the words 'Bow down before the one you serve, you're going to get what you deserve.'"

The timing of turning on the stereo and hearing those words was just too perfect. We both knew it wasn't a coincidence; it was God, speaking through anything that he chose to. After that I had to battle a bit in my mind. I would think, *Maybe that was just a co-incidence. Am I getting crazy, here?* But those "coincidences" just kept happening. Once I opened myself up to the signs that were happening all around, it was impossible to miss them.

relapse

One night after church, I felt the need to clean out my tour bags in my closet to make sure I didn't have any more drugs, and sure enough, I found a big bag of meth. I'd like to say that I flushed it, but that would be lying.

Like a starving man faced with a peanut butter sandwich, I instantly chopped up that speed and snorted it. There was enough there to last me for a week, and I was determined to make it a week of meth.

It was amazing how quickly the drug made me forget all of the good work I had been doing with God. That night, I quit talking to God. I put my Bible away. I firmly resolved to do the rest of my meth, and then quit for good. In a week or so. I just knew without a doubt that would be my last drug binge ever. I would never do any more drugs, ever again, for the rest of my life. For some reason I just knew this was it. But I figured I had to try to hide from God to go on my last binge.

D was awesome through all that stuff. He encouraged me to stick with my commitment to God—and he wasn't even Christian. I kept battling in my mind whether all of this God stuff was real, and D just kept telling me that God was calling me, big time. Over and over, he reassured me that all I needed to do was stick it out and believe because God was real. Perhaps because of his constant support, I hid my last binge from D too, afraid of showing him my true colors.

During my weeklong meth binge, Korn called a band meeting to talk about the approach we were going to take for our eighth album (what became *See You on the Other Side*).

This next album was going to give Korn one of the biggest paydays of our career. Our contract with our record label, Sony, had just ended and now we were free to sign with any label we wanted, which meant millions of dollars for us. This was a huge factor to my hesitation over leaving Korn. It was probably one of the main things that made me go back and forth in my head about quitting. Little did I know that God was also delivering me from my addiction to money too, but it was going to take a bit more time.

leaving korn

As we prepped for our negotiations, I drove up to L.A. one night to meet Pete and Jeff at their office. When I got there, I laid it out for them: I wasn't sure I wanted to be in Korn anymore. I didn't mention God—I just said that I wanted to be with Jennea and I didn't want her to be around my rock 'n' roll lifestyle anymore.

Pete and Jeff didn't like that at all, but they encouraged me to go talk to the band, so I agreed. The meeting was scheduled for the next day, and the more I thought about it, the more I realized that I just didn't have it in me. I couldn't look those guys in the eye and quit. We were a dysfunctional family, but we were still a family, and even though I had been so dissatisfied with the band and with the guys in the band, I still loved them very much, and I couldn't let them down in person. It was just too much for me to deal with at the time.

Instead, I sent them all an e-mail from my hotel, telling them I couldn't tour anymore. Jonathan wrote me back almost instantly. He said:

> Head, we love you. We just want you to be happy. What if you write the new record with us, and then we'll find a guitar player to tour in your spot?

Wow. That was unexpected.

My mind was going in all kinds of different directions when I read that. I never thought any of them would react like that. The solution sounded perfect. I could make music with my friends, be with my daughter, never have to tour, and be a Christian quietly at home. It sounded pretty good to me. I wrote Jonathan back and told him that I had to go home, but that I would think about it and talk to him later.

As I drove back home, a lot of stuff ran through my mind. *Could I stay in Korn? Could I get that fat payday without touring? Could I actually stay home with Jennea and still do music?* It all sounded so good. I stopped thinking and started praying, asking God to show me what to do, and when I got back to Bako, I went straight to Doug's house and asked him his opinion. I figured that, since he was Christian, he would tell me to quit my evil band or something, but he didn't.

Doug instead told me I should go to the band and see if they would be interested in flipping our music around a little bit to make it more positive. I was talking to him about that idea when I got a message unlike any I'd ever had:

> *Go home and write an e-mail to all of the Korn guys and managers and tell them you are quitting the band and there is nothing left to talk about.*

Out of nowhere, I got this strong feeling inside of me. I was hearing God himself. This was way stronger than the words I thought I heard in that hotel room. It was a direct order from God, I could tell. I knew it in my heart.

Without a doubt.

This was no coincidence and this wasn't a sign. This was a message that had come straight from above. The feeling was so overpowering that I had no question about what I was supposed to do. I had to listen to it. The back-and-forth that had been going on in my mind for the last year or so was over in a second. And that huge amount of money that I would've received if I had stayed in Korn suddenly meant nothing after hearing God tell me exactly what to do. And just like that—the war I'd been having inside of me for the last couple of years, the battle over how to live my life and raise my daughter—was finally settled.

I was instantly set free from my double mind, and it felt so good. I marched home and did exactly what I had been told. And as I sat there writing the e-mails to each band member, telling them that I was quitting and giving my life to Christ, I started to feel sad about it, but I knew it had to be done. It was done.

I felt free inside. Like I was finally doing the right thing for Jennea and me.

finally free

Even though I felt released from my personal prison, I still wasn't totally released from my addictions. Instead of talking to God about how I felt about the whole situation, I dove back into the last bit of meth I had. But by then, something was weird about the speed I was doing. I was snorting it, but it didn't seem like I was getting as high as I usually did. I don't know—it was like God was preventing it, showing me that he wasn't going to let me enjoy getting high anymore. My mind was clearer. It was time to be done with drugs forever.

Later that evening, I was sitting at my computer and going through the pages of my Bible, when I felt a peaceful presence hovering over me. Then I felt something hug me—wrapping around me in an embrace. I don't really know how to describe the feeling, other than to say it was like someone poured liquid love into my body and all around me. I had chills all over my whole body—I had never felt anything like that before in my life. I was caught up in total ecstasy.

The high was higher than any drug I'd ever done in my life and I was instantly addicted to it. I looked up and gently said,

"Father?" There was nothing there for me to see, but I could feel his presence so strongly. It was God.

After an experience like that, you would think that I would have gotten up and thrown away every bit of speed I had left. I mean, God opened up heaven for me and let me touch him, but after the experience was over, I ended up doing drugs all night.

At about five in the morning, I finally fell asleep. When I woke up, I felt an urgency to go to my Bible and open it. As soon as I did, I saw a scripture that completely jumped off the page and scared me. It felt like God literally picked up the words from the scripture and shoved them in my face.

It was Ezekiel 18:20—the soul who sins is the one who will die.

I instantly felt the fear of the Lord consume me, and I ran into my closet, grabbed the last bit of speed I had and threw it all in my toilet. After I flushed it, I fell to the ground with my hands in the air and screamed at the top of my lungs, "I am done with drugs forever! God, did I pass the test in time?"

I've never done drugs or alcohol since, and I never will. Just like that, God took away my cravings. I'm not on any wagon, so I will never fall off any wagon. I'm just done. I had tried to quit alcohol and drugs many times while I was in Korn, but I was never able to do it.

On that day all of my addictions ended for good. I knew that, because I now had God in my life, I'd be totally free from my addiction to drugs and alcohol forever. The war was over. I was done running from God. I just wanted to rest in his arms and be free, and that's exactly what I decided to do.

For the next couple of days, God opened up the heavens and let me feel his presence in the same way that he had the night before when I was sitting at my computer. I felt like there were angels all around me, and the Lord was speaking to me through all of them. He helped me understand that he died in my place on the cross two thousand years ago, but he was raised from the dead. Now that I was back with him where I belonged, all the horrible things I did in my past were forgiven and forgotten.

He also guided me with his spirit through scripture and showed me that everyone who follows Christ will be persecuted in some way. It was like he was asking me if I was up for the challenge. I just remember firmly saying, "Yes, Lord, I'll do anything for you." I was so wrecked from the heavenly bliss I was in that nothing else mattered.

He spoke with me in a lot of other ways too. On one of those days I woke up from a nap to see Jennea looking at a book about Pinocchio, and she asked me to read it to her. It didn't take long to realize that God was using that story to speak to me: a toymaker named Geppetto creates Pinocchio, only to find later that Pinocchio has run off with a bunch of wild boys. When Pinocchio gets into trouble and ends up in the stomach of a whale, his creator, Geppetto, saves him. During the rescue, Geppetto is hurt so severely that it seems as though he'd die. But eventually he recovers, and they live happily together.

Given all I'd been through, and how I was opening my heart to God, it was very clear that God was showing me how I was like Pinocchio, and that Jesus (like Geppetto) was saving me from my bad choices that had led me into the belly of the whale.

As I finished reading the story, I felt so much love from God. I felt more freedom than I had ever felt in my entire life.

In fact, I felt so free that I figured everything in my life was going to get easy from then on.

I had no idea how wrong I was.

DISCUSSION QUESTIONS

1. When Head met Eric at the coffee shop, Eric suggested they pray so that Head could ask Jesus *back* into his life. Earlier in this book, Head describes his summer before high school when he asked Jesus into his heart—but he

went back to his old life. If his first prayer was valid, do you think Head really needed to ask Jesus back in? Why or why not?

2. Do you think it was okay for Eric to suggest to Head that he pray? (Head admits feeling a little bit pressured then.) If you were Eric, how would you have handled that morning at the coffee shop?

3. When Head initially struggled with his addictions after becoming a Christian, the person he trusted most to confide in was his friend, D, a non-Christian. In fact, D was a huge encouragement to Head to keep going with his faith when Head was trying to get off speed. What can we as believers learn from D?

4. After Head was getting better, he took D to a church service, then told him afterward to "watch for signs from God." D got into his car and heard lines from a Nine Inch Nails song that freaked him out. Do you believe that God works through things like songs on the radio? Why or why not?

5. Soon after his conversion, Head realized it was time to leave Korn. But with all the millions of dollars he'd lose, it was a huge temptation to stay. You probably haven't been faced with such huge temptations in your life, but describe a time when you felt like you needed to get out of a situation in order for your Christian walk to thrive.

6. At one point toward the end of his addiction, Head discovered that speed wasn't giving him the same pleasure it used to. How does God encourage you to stop doing things that are bad by making them less fun or enjoyable?

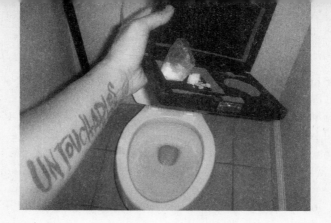

12. the *real* walk of faith

I quit Korn. I completely walked away from everything. Life—as I had known it—was over. That was it.

All at once, I left almost everyone and everything connected to my old life. It was as though my old life had to die so that I could follow the Lord. There was no turning back—and it felt so right. I fell deeply and passionately in love with God, and I made up my mind that he was in control of every part of me from that moment on.

Ever since that intense week when I quit Korn and had my last drug binge, I have dedicated myself to living a life of purity through the power of the Holy Spirit. No high from any drug could compare to the high that God gave me. I'm not saying I'm perfect; I make mistakes and slip up just like everyone does. I just try as best as I can, but there is no way I could do it with my

---

The day that God helped me say goodbye to meth for good was one of the best days of my life. With his help, I flushed everything down the toilet, and I've been clean ever since.

own strength. And when I mess up, I get up, dust my knees off, and keep walking with God.

The Bible says that God is love, and I'm addicted to God's love because he saved me from killing myself with drugs and alcohol. He saved my daughter from losing her dad. He took away all the bad things in my life, and I love God so much for that. He deserves everything that I am, so for the rest of my life, I'm going to try to give God everything I am. And again, I'm not claiming to be some Holy Roller who lives a sin-free life. I mess up all the time, but then I get up and keep walking with God.

I was just so deep in the gutter that the only way I could get out was for God to reveal himself to me, to show me that he's real, and that he really loves me. While I was in the worst time of my life, I felt heaven come down and touch me. Because of that, I'll never be the same. It was the most beautiful feeling in the world. It felt like paradise. It felt like unconditional love. A very intense love that I'd never felt before, and that love is what I'd been really craving my whole life. The high from all the drugs I did could never compare to the high God gave me that day.

Since leaving Korn, I've been totally living by faith, totally relying on God to fill out every major and minor detail in my life. From growing my faith, to recording my music, to helping me raise my kid, to providing money for me to pay the bills and every other provision I need in life.

Now I want to share with you my victories and struggles about living the *real* Christian life, the real walk of faith. Not the phony stuff you sometimes see on TV, but the type of life where we walk with God the same way the disciples in the New Testament walked with Christ.

It's a full-on, risk-filled life that I believe God desires all Christians to live. It's when you completely lay down every part of your life so Christ can live through you.

"I have been crucified with Christ and I no longer live, but Christ lives in me" (Gal. 2:19–20).

When you decide to trust in God that way, you don't take care of yourself anymore—God takes care of you. It isn't easy at first, though; it goes against every logical thing we've ever been taught our whole lives, so some of what I say may sound weird. That's how I felt in the beginning, and I had to overcome a lot of disbelief as I learned about walking this real walk of faith, since it runs counter to the way most people live.

So let's back up and talk about what life was like when I first became a Christian. Let's start with this: when God reached down to me and spoke to me, I really believed in him. He was real to me.

The devil? Not so much. When people would talk about the devil, it just sounded stupid to me. "Ooooh, the devil is gonna come and get me." Real scary, right? But then my ideas about the devil changed. I know now that the devil is real, just like God is real.

Soon after my visitation from God, I had a visitation that was either from the devil, or some form of demon. In fact, anybody who sincerely gives his or her life to Christ will come in contact with the devil eventually. I know that sort of thing may sound weird, or even stupid, to some of you, but it's true. Honestly, it sounded weird and stupid to *me*. Until, that is, I experienced it for myself.

demonic attacks

After my final drug binge, I was really tired and ready to crash hard. I wanted to crash for a long time. I headed to my room, crawled into bed, and went to sleep almost immediately. Usually I would sleep for hours after a binge like this, but I had only been asleep for a few minutes before I woke up. I looked around and saw the outlines of all the furniture in my room. Everything was still and quiet.

I had been really tired when I went to sleep, so there was no reason for me to be awake. At first, I thought I should go check on Jennea or something. I started to get out of my bed when it hit me:

I couldn't move.

I was completely paralyzed.

I. Couldn't. Move.

I freaked. I didn't understand what was happening to me— I just couldn't move my body at all, no matter how hard I tried. I tried to scream out to God, but what came out of my mouth was not my voice. My voice had been replaced by a deep, scratchy noise. It sounded unearthly, like something from *The Exorcist*.

My eyes went wide. I freaked again.

I lay there for a moment, my mind racing, fear pulsating through me. I tried to remember the embrace of liquid love I had felt earlier, but it seemed so far away. This was a totally different embrace. It was an embrace of hate. Of fear. Of some kind of evil I'd never felt before.

And then, just like that, it was gone.

I leapt out of my bed and looked around in disbelief about what had just happened. I had done drugs for years, and nothing like this had *ever* happened to me before, so I knew it wasn't drug related. It wasn't just in my head. I could literally feel the evil that was holding me down.

This was real.

I immediately called a new Christian friend I'd met who knew about this sort of stuff. We talked for a bit and he helped calm me down by telling me that the next time it happened, I needed to do what Jesus had done: I needed to tell the devil to get behind me. Maybe because of all the horror movies I watched, I never believed in the existence of a devil or demons or anything like that; now I was being tormented by evil I'd never experienced before. But Christ was in my life now, and I couldn't let the devil—or whatever it was—push me around. I went back to bed, confident this time that, if it happened again, I would be ready for it.

I soon dozed off, and again, about ten minutes into my sleep, I woke up, and again, I was totally paralyzed with that same *Exorcist* voice I had earlier, only this time I said in my deep rasp, "Get behind me, Satan."

Nothing happened.

I panicked. Why wasn't it working?

I laid there for a little while, freaking out inside, fighting this battle in my mind. I was scared to death that what my friend had suggested wasn't working, but I had to keep believing in God, believing that he was real. Eventually it went away and I went back to sleep, but it happened again. And again. And again. And every time the same thing: I woke up paralyzed and tried to tell the devil where to go, but nothing changed. Each time I had to sit through mind-numbing terror for a little while until the paralysis ended, then I would go back to sleep only to wake up again and have everything repeat.

Coming off my binge, sleep was the one thing I was looking for, but now this demon or devil was trying to scare me so badly that I wouldn't want to go back to sleep. And if I didn't go to sleep, where would I turn? Speed, of course. The devil was using fear as a way to try to keep me on speed. He wanted me to be in bondage to the drug, because if I stayed addicted, I would keep hurting my daughter and myself and eventually die.

But these were all conclusions I came to months after the fact. At the time, I didn't have the slightest idea what was going on. All I knew was that it had something to do with God and the devil; the feeling was just too evil *not* to be from the devil. I was touched by good, and then touched by evil—all in the same week. I didn't see either one; I just felt the presence of both strongly.

I had read a little bit about Jesus casting demons out of people in the Bible, so I figured maybe that's what was happening to me, but in truth, I didn't know then and I still don't know today. Only God knows what really went on that day, but whatever it was, it was evil and it had a mind of its own.

The next morning, I called the pastor at that church where I was saved, Pastor Ron Vietti from VBF (it stands for Valley Bible Fellowship, but everyone there calls it VBF), and asked if he and his wife could come out to my house and pray. I was pretty freaked out, so I asked them if they could come over quickly, and a couple of hours later Pastor Ron and his wife, Debbie, showed up. They went through every room in the house, commanding evil spirits to leave. It was all still pretty strange to me because I had never seen anything like it, but at the same time, I didn't want to get paralyzed again, so I just went with it.

That night, I didn't really feel like sleeping in my bed because that's where it had happened the night before. I guess I was a little scared that it would happen again, even though Pastor Ron and Debbie had prayed. More importantly, though, I knew God was in me; I knew that Christ's power was bigger and better. I kept that in mind as I put Jennea to bed. I lay down with her to help her get to sleep, and then. . . .

It happened again.

Total paralysis.

An instant replay of the night before.

But for some reason, I didn't feel any fear this time. Not even in the least. I surprised myself, because I was more annoyed than anything else, but my fear was gone. Instead, I just laughed at how ridiculous it was (at least this time, when I laughed, my voice didn't have that *Exorcist* quality to it).

I laughed again and said, "Let me go, Satan."

Boom. Just like that it was gone, and it's never happened again.

Since I had that experience, I have done a little bit of studying about the devil and demons so I could understand more about what was really going on with me. I found out that they are spiritual beings (fallen angels) that are real, evil, and in the world today.

Learning this later on when I was ready for it was incredibly eye-opening, but at the time that it happened, I was still a long way from being prepared for this stuff. Until I had that experience, I had lived my whole life thinking that everything about the devil was stupid, but my whole belief system got turned around when I experienced it for myself. That wouldn't be the last time my belief system got turned around.

a new lifestyle

After those episodes, Pastor Ron and Debbie became friends of mine, and I started hanging out at VBF a lot. The church had its own private school, so I grabbed Jennea out of public school and enrolled her at the VBF school. It was around then that I first told Jennea I had quit Korn to be at home with her and to live for God.

She was very excited that I would be able to be with her all the time, and for the first time ever, I felt like a good dad. I had been through so much with her, and it felt so good to not only hope, but to know for sure that everything was going to be all right.

In addition to this major change in our routine and Jennea's school, I also started making some lifestyle adjustments. I prayed in front of Jennea and asked God to show her a miracle by taking away my urge to use cuss words. For the most part, he did

perform that miracle, but I am human, and I still do slip sometimes.

After some reflection, I decided to put all of the gold and plat-
inum Korn awards that were hanging on the walls of my house
in my garage. While those awards made me proud, I needed to
move on and it helped not to see that stuff every day. In addition, I also threw away most of the music that I had listened to
until my awakening—not because I thought it was devil's music
or anything—but because I wanted to listen to music that would
attract the presence of God since that's all I craved in life.

Also, whenever the doors were open for church, I went. Sunday morning. Monday night. Tuesday night. Wednesday night.
I was there three, four times a week. I was doing all I could to
get to know God better. Every time I was at a church service, so
many tears would fall from my eyes. I've learned that's one of
the ways the Lord shows me that he's with me. It's like those are
his tears because he's crying right through me.

The thing that totally amazed me is that the place where I
felt the presence of God the most was in my own home. I had
very intimate moments with God at home, and I quickly realized that God didn't live in a building called a church. Though
I didn't fully understand it yet, I was starting to realize that he
lived in me and was everywhere I was—just like Kevin's mom
had said when I was thirteen. Still, I loved going to church and
being around people who had walked with God for a long time.
All I wanted to do was learn as much as I could about God, and
other people were a great way to do that.

making amends

Around then, God led me to make a list of all the people that
I had hurt while I was on drugs so I could contact all of them
and ask for forgiveness. He also wanted me to make things right

with all of my enemies. That was kind of hard, but God was in control of my life and whatever he said went, so I made the list. Besides, he showed me that making peace with everyone was part of my inner healing process. And I needed healing deep where I knew only God could reach.

While this healing process was deep, up to this point there was one part of my previous life that hadn't left me: depression. For years, I had been battling depression, even from the early times in Korn. It was this dark, heavy cloud that would come over me from time to time and just hang there, impossible to escape. I tried to forget about it and mask it by doing drugs or drinking beer, but once I became a Christian, I just assumed God would take that depression from me.

He didn't.

For the first few months after I embraced Jesus, I didn't feel as depressed because I was so high on my new life, sort of like I was a newborn baby, but the depression was still lingering in the background, and little did I know that one day it would come back—with a vengeance.

A few weeks after I got saved, I started to feel like God wanted me to make a public statement about my Christianity, so I asked Pastor Ron if I could give my testimony at VBF during a Sunday service. He told me to pray about it to make sure that was what God wanted me to do; he didn't want anyone pressuring me into it—it had to be my decision. I firmly told him God wanted me to, so we set up a date.

DISCUSSION QUESTIONS

1. After Head had been set free from drugs once and for all, he talks about living "a full-on, risk-filled life that I believe God desires all Christians to live," like the disciples lived in the New Testament. Does that describe your

life? If not, what would it take for your life to be like that?

2. Head experienced a demonic attack soon after his conversion. Do you know anyone who's experienced such an attack?

3. One of the lifestyle changes Head attempted was cussing less. Is this an issue you find among Christians you know?

4. Another thing Head did was get rid of all the music he'd been listening to before his conversion. How do you feel about Christians listening to secular music? Does the musical style matter? Just the lyrics? What about the artist's lifestyle or public image?

5. Head also decided to make amends with his enemies and to ask forgiveness of every person he ever hurt. Where in the Bible can you find passages that relate to this very subject?

13. i go public

A few days later, I called KRAB-FM, the local rock radio station in Bakersfield, which was huge on playing Korn. I felt like God wanted me to use this station to announce that I was leaving the band, that I had become a Christian, and that I was going to give my testimony at the church. I called up KRAB and wound up going into the studio pretty quickly to do an interview with them. I told them what was going on, about my upcoming testimony at VBF, and that was that.

So I thought.

The next morning, someone from the church called me and said that CNN and MTV had both contacted the church, wanting to do interviews about me quitting Korn and giving my life to Christ. I guess the news of my conversion had hit the Internet, and now people all over the world were freaking out over it.

This shot of a dove was taken completely by accident right after our group's baptism. It was a miraculous sign from God that I was exactly where I was supposed to be.

I freaked out too. I wasn't trying to make a big scene or get a bunch of publicity for myself; I was just trying to follow God. I thought that, if I could get even a few Korn fans into the church on Sunday, they would have a chance to meet Christ like I had.

Apparently the Korn guys were pretty angry about my announcement because Pete and Jeff were in the process of negotiating a new record deal for them and my announcement made it a lot harder for them to do that. While they were talking to record companies, here I was telling the world that I had quit the band and was living for God.

But the reality was that I wasn't doing things Korn's way anymore. As much as I loved those guys, my only job now was to listen to God and try to be completely obedient to him. That's just the way it had to be.

As word spread, things started to get crazy in the media, and there was all this fuss about my conversion. People were making this a big deal, much bigger than I had imagined. I was just sitting at home, tripping out about all this madness, when Pastor Ron called me and said that a group of people from the church was going to Israel the day after I was scheduled to give my testimony, and they had a free extra ticket. He asked me if I would be interested in going to Israel and checking out where Jesus had lived while he was on Earth. I didn't really know if I wanted to, but I felt like God really wanted me to go, so I agreed.

Another thing happened around this time: I felt the urge to get tattoos of my faith. While I was in Korn, I wasn't all tatted down like a lot of rock stars. I only had four:

- The logo from *Issues* on my arm.

- A picture of a guy who had peeled off his skin and was holding it and looking at it. It's like the guy was looking at his past. This one made me think about starting over when D and I got sober right before I recorded *Untouchables*.

- The Korn logo on my lower back.

- "Jennea" on my neck, and the name of the child who Rebekah and I gave up for adoption.

Now, though, I felt God telling me to make my body a statement of faith, so I hit up a tattoo place and started getting inked up. For my first one, I went straight for the neck and put "Matthew 11:28" there. It's the scripture that kept popping up all over the place when I first got saved: "Come to me all who are weary and burdened and I will give you rest." Then I got "Jesus" tattooed on my right hand, with one letter on each finger. I had the tattoo artist write it on my hand so it faced me—I figured since I'm right-handed, I'd probably start all my actions with my right hand, so I wanted the Lord's name to be the first thing I saw, no matter what I was doing. Then I got "Matthew 6:19" on the other side of my neck. That scripture says to not store up treasures on earth, but to build up heavenly riches. I got that one because God set me free from my addiction to money.

testimony time

At last that Sunday rolled around when I had decided I was going to tell my church—and the rest of the world through the media that had gathered there—that I quit Korn and was now a Christian. I've got to be honest: I was pretty nervous. Part of that was probably because I didn't know what I was going to say. I had no idea. I didn't write anything down or bounce any ideas off friends. I just winged it.

Well, that's not totally true, since I did prepare for it with a lot of prayer. I prayed that God would reveal to me what I needed to say, because there were just so many cameras and people there—even fans of Korn, who'd driven a long way to come see me give my testimony. I also saw some old friends there. Richard, the singer from LAPD, was there, and Korn's wardrobe assistant, Lesley. D and his family came (in fact, D's son gave his life to the Lord that morning). My parents were there, too, and my brother and sister-in-law and a few other relatives of mine. There were also a lot of other people who I used to hang out with when I was a kid there to support me. I took a lot of encouragement from all the support I had there.

On the way to the church to give my testimony, I felt the Lord tell me what he wanted me to say to the people. But what *he* wanted me to talk about, I didn't want to talk about. God wanted me to talk about speed. He wanted me to tell the whole world that I had been addicted to meth, and how he had set me free from that addiction.

Up to this point, I hadn't really told anyone other than D about my speed addiction. It was still more or less my secret. While I had told a couple of the guys who were helping me learn more about how to walk with God, they were all former druggies, so I felt I could trust them and didn't feel embarrassed around them.

But there were a lot more than four people in that church. In the end, more than thirteen thousand people showed up to hear my testimony that morning—not to mention the potential millions of others who would hear or see it on CNN, MTV, and whatever other news stations and newspapers around the world that would carry the story.

Basically, God was telling me to tell the whole world that I was a loser.

That was a pretty scary thought, but God reminded me my whole story was about him setting me free from that prison, not about me being ashamed at myself.

So that was how I ended up telling the whole world that I had spent almost the last two years of my life addicted to speed. With God's help that morning I confessed my sins to the world. It never even occurred to me that most people sort of expect rock stars to be totally hooked on drugs anyway. To me, I was sharing my dirtiest secret with the world—all because God had told me to do so. It was a truly humbling moment.

After the whole thing was over, I was suddenly very thankful that I was leaving for Israel the next day.

my israel experience

While the timing of my trip to Israel could not have been better because of the media circus, I was incredibly excited for my own reasons. I was going to a place that I had never been, and I had been to a lot of places. This was going to be a different trip, though—no band, no guitars, no partying. I was just going as Brian, not as a rock star.

As we were preparing to leave, Pastor Ron got a phone call from his secretary back home at the church. MTV had called, and they wanted to send a camera crew with us to Israel, so they could film our trip and everything that we did. Apparently they were filming a show about spirituality, and they wanted me to be a part of it.

I don't know why, but I agreed. I just felt like it was a chance for me to make God look good, and I hadn't done much of that up to that point in my life. In addition, I was just so amazed at the idea that I would be walking around in the same places where Jesus had walked and I wanted to share that sense of wonder with others.

I wish I could say that everything was really mellow on that trip, but I can't. Throughout the whole trip, I experienced mood issues with a lot of anger that came and went. I figured that because I had just gotten saved, it meant I could be totally perfect now. I wasn't going to mess up anymore or want to do bad stuff. But it just wasn't happening, and my frustration resulted in a lot of anger. I didn't understand then that it doesn't work like that.

It didn't help that I had a camera in my face the whole time I was there. I thought it would be easy to have them follow me around, but it got in the way as I tried to come to terms with the significance of the trip. I had to do an interview at every stop we made, and it was starting to irritate me—perhaps because I could feel the dark cloud of depression waiting just off the horizon.

In spite of those problems, I still had a lot of very blissful feelings while I was in the Holy Land. As I walked through places where Jesus had walked, I could sense his presence around me, comforting me and helping me through this process. I could feel the Lord holding me, like I had held Jennea when she was a newborn baby. It was this peaceful feeling that God loved me and was taking care of me.

I also wrote some song lyrics while I was there, and I really felt like God was leading me to write a prophetic song to 50 Cent. One thing to keep in mind before you read these lyrics is that while I believe these words were inspired by God, written through me to 50 Cent, more importantly I believe the words carry a message to everyone else in this generation, including myself. A message straight to us from God's heart.

Here are some of the lyrics to a song I wound up calling "A Cheap Name":

Wisdom comes through suffering
Tell me why'd you let him give you a cheap name?

It's time to come home
Playtime's over now

It's my world
It's my plan
It's my sea
It's my land
It's my moon
They're my stars
You're my mind
You're my heart
What's your choice?
What's your role?
You're my life
You're my soul
You're my son
You're my seed
We're one love
Come home, please

jordan river baptism

In addition to writing my first verses of song lyrics, I got the chance to be baptized in the Jordan River, the same river where Jesus was baptized. Now at this point, I had only been a Christian a couple of months, and I didn't know much about how to walk with Jesus. All I knew was that I was supposed to believe, and as a result I had many misconceptions about following Jesus.

One area of confusion surrounded the baptism itself. I knew that baptism symbolized being reborn as a new person, but for some reason, I believed that, when I was baptized, every bad thing, every bad feeling, every bad thought was going to fall off of me forever when I came out of the water. I thought that you go under as yourself and you come up changed.

I thought that when I went under, that old, angry, depressed me was going to be dead forever. I didn't understand that it was going to be this long, off-and-on, painful process that I would have to go through over the next couple years.

All these expectations put a lot of pressure on that moment.

When we got to the baptism spot, there were a bunch of cameras set up from CNN and Fox News and places like that, not to mention the MTV camera that was already following me around everywhere. It was very nerve-racking, because that was such a personal moment for me, and to have it all recorded on tape made me nervous, but I felt like God had set it all up. I wasn't ashamed to show everyone in the world how much I loved my God and how sorry I was for my past. I just went along for the whole press ride.

I waited in line for about ten minutes before I was baptized. I cried the whole time. I was overwhelmed with emotion, and I felt the Lord right there with me. I was putting my old self to death. A new man would rise out of the water.

When it finally was my turn to be baptized, I started walking deeper into the water, and I was shaking and shivering because it was so cold. Just before Pastor Ron and the other guys dunked me, I asked them to hold me down underneath the water longer than most people because I probably had more junk to wash away. They laughed and agreed.

When I finally came out of the water, I felt awesome, and the one thing that I really wanted was to go and chill for a bit. That wasn't so easy because I had to do interviews with the news stations. I even told one news anchor that I believed my evil spirits got washed away in the water. The guy just looked at me like I was out of my mind. And maybe I was out of my mind in some ways, but the one way I was in my right mind was getting baptized in the name of Christ. That was the best decision I've ever made.

Even though I had some confusion about how baptisms work, it was an awesome experience that had an unspeakable impact on my life. I did feel the presence of the Lord change me that day, but instead of being the end, it was merely the beginning. The baptism was just the first step of my transformative process.

a dove in the photo

Shortly after the group had been baptized, we shared another amazing moment together. In the Bible, after Jesus was baptized, the Holy Spirit came down from heaven in the shape of a dove and descended on Jesus. Not long after our baptism, we were all in a room together when suddenly another member of the group had his digital camera accidentally go off. He wasn't trying to take a picture, it just happened unintentionally.

When he went to take a look at the picture, sitting in the exact center of the frame was a dove. Apparently a dove had flown into the room from the outside at the same moment that his camera went off, and he had inadvertently snapped a perfectly straight picture of this dove.

Of course, we were all overwhelmed because it matched so closely with what God had done for Jesus when *he* had been baptized. We were all convinced that this was how God chose to show us that he was with us. It was an amazing occurrence and it set the perfect tone for the rest of the trip and beyond.

DISCUSSION QUESTIONS

1. Head decided it was finally time to tell the world he quit Korn and drugs and was now a believer in Christ. Have

you ever given a public testimony about how you came to faith in Jesus? If not, do you think you're ready to ask your youth leader or a Christian adult you trust how to do it?

2. Head talks a lot about the media and how they made certain aspects of his testimony more difficult. Do you think it was good that he had cameras there to help spread the word, or do you think it would have been better if his experience were more personal?

3. Head also got baptized in the Jordan River. Have you ever been baptized? If so, was it when you were a baby or later on? When do you think a Christian should be baptized, and how? What does the Bible have to say?

4. At the end of the chapter, Head talks about how the accidental photo of the dove helped everyone know they were in the right place. Have you ever had God send you a clear sign that you were doing the right thing?

14. winning battles,
winning souls

When I got back from Israel, the only thing I wanted to do was get to know God better so I could do whatever he wanted me to do. And since one of the ways God speaks to people is through the Bible, I made up my mind to start devouring my Bible.

As it turned out, there were a couple of problems with that plan. The first was that I often had a hard time sitting still long enough to really read the Bible. The other problem was that much of the time I was reading I didn't understand what it said—and when I did understand it, I didn't always believe it. To solve these issues, I started reading the Bible in little bits, asking God to help me believe and understand it, and spent the rest of my time working on some solo music. I figured that along

My reunion with Kevin. It was cool to tell him about the role that he played in my decision to follow Christ.

the way, I would also talk with people who could help me understand it and support my desire to learn everything I could about God.

Around this time, I felt led by God to do a thorough exploration of my master closet, where I used to hide my drugs. I felt as though he wanted me to make sure there wasn't even one pill or straw left in there. Although I had gone through it before, it was a huge walk-in closet that had two levels to hang the clothes, so it was easy to miss things.

On this go-round, I made sure to look through every square inch of that closet and, sure enough, I found another huge bag of speed I had hidden months before in a first-aid kit, of all places. I thought I would never see meth in front of my face again after I flushed it all down the toilet, but there I was, alone at home, with a bag of speed.

Bad thoughts instantly came to me.

Nobody will ever know.

I can just do a little bit and then throw the rest away.

One last binge, and then I'll quit forever, no matter what.

"No!" I screamed. I instantly put the bag of meth on the shelf in the closet, walked out of the room, and started praying.

"Oh, God, help me! I gotta be done with this! I'm not going to be a slave to it anymore! God, please, give me the strength to do the right thing!"

I had recently gotten a new tattoo on my hand; it was the scripture reference for Philippians 4:13. I knew that tattoo would come in handy. I quoted the verse out loud:

"I can do all things through Christ who strengthens me."

Suddenly, I felt strong enough to go back in the closet to grab the speed and throw it out. Right then, I found out how powerful the scriptures really are (Heb. 4:12). In fact, the Lord gave me so much strength that I got another idea. I decided to get my camera and take pictures of myself throwing the meth away. I wanted to remember this huge day of victory.

Up until then, I had *believed* I was delivered from drugs, but that day I really *knew* I was delivered from them. In that one moment, the Lord showed me how much strength he had given me and what I was capable of as long as I had him on my side.

vicious backlash

After that encounter with the speed, I really tried to focus on praying, reading my Bible, and writing music. I tried my best to stay out of the press and to avoid paying too much attention to the media, since I had heard that a lot of people were making fun of my conversion.

While no one was going to say anything that would make me change my mind about God, occasionally I would hear bad things about myself in the media and it was always hard to listen to. When I first decided to go public, I knew I would be mocked, so it came as no surprise. But I had no idea how vicious it would get.

It all began when the lead singer of Tool made a statement that he had given his life to Christ, and MTV called me and did an interview with me about it. I said all this great stuff about how this was exactly what God was doing, and that in the future, there would be a lot of musicians getting saved. I talked about how beautiful it was that he had been saved, and how supportive I was of his decision. I just tried to make it clear how happy I was that someone else from the music world had been helped by God in the same way I had been.

Not long after I gave the interview, I found out that it was just a hoax, and I walked right into it. Things got worse when Jonathan started saying some stuff in the press about my conversion. In turn, I said some stuff back about him, and it started to get pretty pointless. I decided then to stay out of the spotlight for a while.

But behind the scenes, the drama didn't stop. I sent some messed up e-mails to my managers because I was bitter about what Jonathan had said. I just couldn't let go of the anger I felt toward them even though I knew I was wrong to be feeling it. To my shame, I have to admit that I harassed them for a couple weeks before I abandoned the bitterness. Looking back on it now, it was such a tough time for me to deal with all the things going on. I just had all these emotions going on in me at once, and a lot of them weren't good, but I didn't always know how to deal with them.

For some reason, I started to feel like I was in competition with my band, like I was special because God had chosen me or something. As I stepped back and looked at myself, it started to become very clear to me that I had a lot of issues I needed to address if I was ever going to be a happy person. As much as I wanted my problems to wash off me, I had to realize that nothing was going to magically disappear right away.

reuniting with kevin

Not everything about my past was hard to deal with, and I made a point to seek out the people who'd had a positive impact on my life. Around then, a friend suggested that I try to contact Kevin and his family to tell them about how they'd helped to put me on the path to Jesus when I was younger. I thought it was a good idea, so the next day I drove to East Bakersfield and stopped by Kevin's old house to see if his parents still lived there.

To my surprise, Kevin's mom, Terry, opened the door. I told her who I was, and of course, she remembered me. She invited me in, and we sat and talked for a while. Terry had already heard the news that I had given my life to Christ, but what she didn't know was the role her family had played in my conversion. I told her how I had asked Jesus into my heart after she explained it to me and how that experience was the main reason I had come to Christ recently. Her family had been my first sign way back when, and even though I had missed it then, their role was undeniable now. When she heard that, she was overjoyed; she had no idea she had impacted me in that way.

It was an incredible afternoon, but our time together didn't end there. Soon after that, I invited Kevin and his family over to my house for a party I threw for Jennea. While we were celebrating, Kevin and I hung out for the first time since that summer when we were friends. In speaking to him and his family, it was clear that they were all happy to know they had influenced my life in such a positive way.

healing with rebekah

At the same time that I was reconnecting with Kevin and his family, so many other crazy things were happening. I was so excited to be a follower of Christ that I loved doing anything God told me to do. I would pray as much as I could every day, and God would often put certain people in my heart to pray for.

One of them was D. Ever since I told him about my addiction, D had played a major role in helping me through my struggle. All the while I just kept talking to D about how God was so real, and although he believed me, he just wasn't ready to become a Christian. Understanding his reluctance, I kept talking to him about God.

Shortly thereafter, I met this girl named Ashley who had been a huge fan of Korn and had started coming to VBF. We started talking about the Lord, and she ended up inviting him into her heart. After some discussion, she decided that she also wanted to get baptized.

Another person I had started praying for was my old friend, JC, who I hadn't really spoken to in a while. One day, not long after my trip to Israel, he called me out of the blue and told me he had been arrested for something minor and needed someone to bail him out. While he was in jail, there was a guy who followed him around and talked constantly about Jesus. After listening to him and talking to me, JC decided he wanted to know Christ like I did, so I bailed him out of jail and told him about everything the Lord had done for me. Then *he* wanted to be baptized.

With these three new believers at my side, I called up the church and talked to a pastor named Pastor Jim, and he came over and helped me baptize all three of them in my pool.

But D and JC weren't the only people from my past who were benefiting from the Lord's love.

God was working in Rebekah's life as well.

Since we'd split up, she had been in Hawaii spending most of her time being massively hooked on speed. One day, she was at the beach, just standing on a pier, when she realized that her life was out of control and she needed help.

Rebekah had been raised as a Jehovah's Witness, so she believed in God, and she decided it was time to call out to him. Standing on that pier in Hawaii, Rebekah looked to the sky and said a quiet prayer asking God to help her.

Sometimes God's help doesn't look exactly like help. A few days later, she got arrested and was placed in a drug rehab program, where she was able to start dealing with her addiction.

Shortly after I got back from Israel, I felt like I should take Jennea out to Hawaii to see her mother. When we got there, Rebekah told us about asking God for help, and we told her how different our lives were after deciding to give our lives to Christ.

After telling Rebekah all this stuff about our lives as Christians, we asked her if she wanted to ask Christ into her heart like we did, and she said she did. We all said a prayer together, and Rebekah invited Christ into her heart. It was so cool. After all that craziness that Rebekah, Jennea, and I had been through, here we were, the three of us, praying together. It was a complete miracle.

When we were finished, she said she felt different—so light, and totally happy. She hadn't felt that way in a long time. I also finally had the chance to apologize to Rebekah for all the pain that I put her through. She apologized too, and just like that God helped us put years of pain behind us for good.

DISCUSSION QUESTIONS

1. After all the great stuff God had shown Head since his conversion, Head actually finds more speed in his closet. But instead of taking it like he's tempted to do, Head prays to God then recites out loud Philippians 4:13— "I can do all things through Christ who strengthens me"—and he's able to flush the drugs down the toilet. What can we learn from Head's victory?

2. Our culture is pretty hip to what Christians say and do— even TV shows have hypocritical "Christianese" down pat. It can be pretty embarrassing. Head experienced this first hand after he left Korn, as many fans and fellow musicians ridiculed him for his conversion. Do you think Christians deserve such treatment? Why or why not?

3. Head reunites with Kevin, the childhood friend who first shared Christ with him back before high school. Can you think of Christians who you've lost touch with who

were instrumental to your spiritual growth? If so, here's a challenge: Do your best to track them all down and tell them how much their efforts meant to your walk.

4. Head talks about how God helped him to heal his troubled past with Rebekah, even though they still were not meant to be husband and wife. Have you had any struggles with friends that God has helped to heal?

15. tongues and trust

The trip to Hawaii and my conversation with Rebekah only made my faith that much stronger. As I thought about what he had done for the three of us in such a short period of time, it really was nothing short of remarkable.

When Jennea and I returned from Hawaii, I started praying even more, telling God that I wanted to have more of him in my life. I was so hungry and desperate for more of him, and I wanted to get as close to him as I could. It continuously amazed me that the one and only eternal God was so *real*, and he knew who I was. I mean, he actually knew my *name*.

I did whatever I could do to learn more, and everywhere I went, every person I met, I looked for new things about the Lord. I kept begging him to reveal more of himself to me, and he answered my prayers when he had a new friend of mine named Nathan take me to this other church across town named

When I opened myself up to the Lord, I also opened my body up to a whole lot of new ink.

Grace Assembly of God. On the way there, Nathan was telling me about the church, and he said it was Pentecostal.

"Penny who?" I said.

I didn't know what Pentecostal meant, but I was so on fire for God that it didn't matter where I went; I just wanted more of God.

Man, this church was pretty trippy. These people were very passionate about God. It was awesome.

But weird.

And here's the thing that really tripped me out: they all spoke in tongues, or what some Christians call a prayer language. It's also called praying in the Spirit (1 Cor. 14:4, Jude 20). It's like God giving you the words to pray, even though you don't understand the words (1 Cor. 14:2).

At first, I found the whole speaking in tongues thing really strange, but I was so excited about God that I stopped caring if it seemed strange. To be totally honest, the whole thing completely freaked me out because I didn't understand it at all. But I had this burning desire inside of me to find out if it was real, or if it was just stuff people did to try to act spiritual.

I stayed through the service, and afterward I met the pastor—Eddie Summers. Pastor Eddie gave me his number and told me to call him during the week to talk about being *over*-filled with the Spirit. Initially I didn't understand him; I thought I had been filled with the Holy Spirit when I got baptized in Israel.

However, I was really hungry for God, so I called Pastor Eddie later that week and took a trip down to his office. After we talked for a while, he prayed with me and asked God to *over*-fill me with his Holy Spirit, suggesting that I ask too.

While I was praying, I felt my stomach suddenly contract, and I knew that God had done something inside me. I didn't know *what*, exactly, but I knew something was different. I felt it. Pastor Eddie started talking about that prayer language, and how God wanted to give me one of my own, so that I could use it to speak to him alone.

He showed me in scripture what it meant (1 Cor. 14), and after I saw it in the Bible, I believed him. He explained that initially it would sound kind of weird, but I would hear syllables come out of my mouth that didn't sound like English or any other language, kind of like a baby trying to talk for the first time. It was very weird to me, but I felt God in it, so I decided to give it a try right there in Pastor Eddie's office.

This was what came out: *see-alafol-abaha*. It wasn't much, but it was something and we were all stoked. Pastor Eddie suggested that I go home, ask God to give me more words to my prayer language, and wait on him. He would make it grow in time.

So that's what I did. I wanted all that God had for me, and I didn't care what I had to do to get it, no matter how weird it seemed on the outside. And this stuff was weird! But in the Bible, it says that God uses the foolish things of the world to confound the wise (1 Cor. 1:27), and with that in mind, I was ready to jump straight into the foolishness (but I did have a hard time believing that babbling in some crazy language would actually grow my faith).

In spite of my skepticism, it worked, and after enough praying to God, I started speaking in my prayer language. I was talking to God in an unknown tongue, and I could feel it working inside me, building me up (1 Cor. 14:4, Jude 20). I couldn't explain it; I just knew it was happening.

church conflict

Before I went to the Pentecostal Church, I had spent a lot of time working with Pastor Ron. He had really taken me under his wing and in a short time had taught me a lot about the Bible, becoming a spiritual mentor for me. Once I had my breakthrough with speaking in tongues, I was so excited that I called him up to tell him about it.

Unfortunately, he wasn't as excited as I was. He asked me how I knew that the language I was using was from God. I said I didn't know; I just wanted more of God. As Ron explained, tongues were not something that everyone believed in, but I had no idea this was the case. No one had ever explained to me that there were different ways to get more of God, and while I was really surprised, I was also pretty bummed.

During the conversation with Ron, I let him know that I had also been studying the Bible with Pastor Eddie, and I was saddened and surprised when Ron told me that if I kept studying the Bible with Pastor Eddie, he couldn't mentor me. While it might have seemed that this was just a ploy to keep me at VBF, I knew this wasn't the case. He just didn't want me to get confused. He understood the risk of having different spiritual mentors, and though he loved me and meant well, he recognized that speaking in tongues just wasn't something they did at VBF.

This conflict was difficult for me to understand, since after all, tongues were right there in the Bible. However, this experience with tongues became an abrupt introduction into the realities of modern-day Christianity—mainly that there are lots of different church denominations. Different denominations believe the same basic things, but between them are many little differences that ultimately define what each denomination believes. All Christian churches believe Jesus Christ was the Son of God who died for our sins, but beneath that there are a number of other areas where we disagree. One such area is speaking in tongues.

Here's my opinion on speaking in tongues: if you want to have the most faith you can have on this earth, learn to pray in tongues. If you find it too weird, don't pray in tongues. It's just that simple. It all comes down to personal choice, just like everything else in life. God will love you the same whether you pray in tongues or not.

But when I got involved with God, I didn't know any of this stuff. All I knew was that I loved the Lord and I had learned from the Bible that tongues were a great way to communicate with him. Nevertheless, I had to make a decision between Pastor Ron's mentorship and speaking in tongues.

It was a difficult decision. I felt like the Lord had led me to both places, so I couldn't decide *what* to do. For the time being, I decided to stay at VBF and stop trying to speak in my prayer language. As much as I wanted to get more of God in my life, the whole thing seemed to be causing all this confusion, and I didn't want to get confused.

But just as I reached this conclusion, something funny kept happening: I kept running into people who told me about speaking in tongues, and how it was the way a Christian could build up his faith. They told me about how speaking in tongues would completely empower me to kill off my old ways, and some random people even sent me a book (through VBF) about praying in tongues called *The Walk of the Spirit—The Walk of Power* by Dave Roberson (you can get it for free on his Web site).

With all of these people calling me toward tongues, I was still confused about the whole thing, but I felt like these run-ins were not a coincidence. It seemed like God wanted to help me deepen my faith with signs like this, like he was trying to help me open up another path to my spirituality. I decided to try some more of my prayer language, since it was becoming clear to me that God wanted me to do it. I started doing it by myself again at home, asking God to develop my prayer language. I figured that, if God was the only one who knew I was doing it, then it wouldn't cause a fuss.

time for a change

Jennea and I had both grown really close to Pastor Ron and Debbie. My little girl was doing really well in school there, and

I was learning about God with Pastor Ron's help. But in some ways VBF had begun to overwhelm me. For one thing, there were a lot of people in that church, and while that can be a good thing, it also meant that a lot of them were trying to help me in my walk. Everyone meant well, but I was just getting so much outside advice that I couldn't take it all in. In addition, because I was famous, I kind of felt like I was the church mascot and the setup started to make me anxious.

The whole situation made me wonder if I was even supposed to be at VBF anymore. I couldn't shake these thoughts, so I prayed about it and the Lord showed me he was leading me to leave VBF. The Bible says that the Holy Spirit teaches me all things (1 John 2:27), and it was time for me to go into seclusion so I could learn what God wanted me to learn.

At the same time I was having my doubts about VBF, I was praying about a much different matter: music. For a while, I had been thinking about music and the role it would play in my new life. After a whole lot of prayer, I came to believe that God was telling me that he was going to use me to do music for him. My music was no longer mine; it was God's. From everything I was feeling as I prayed to him, I thought he wanted me to start making music for him as soon as possible.

By that same token, I also felt like he wanted to get me out of Bako soon. It just wasn't where I needed to be, and I knew it. There was too much past there and too many distractions. The only problem was that I didn't know where to go or what God wanted me to do, so I prayed.

trusting in god isn't always easy

Like I said before: I had given God my entire life. It was up to him to take care of me now. It was up to him to point me in the right direction. I had to rely totally on him. Even so, a lot of my doubts remained. Thoughts would flash through my mind: *What if God only cleaned me up to be a good dad? What if I wasn't supposed to leave Korn?*

Some days I just straight-up panicked. It was all so new to me, and I know now that the devil was in the mix somewhere, trying to make me doubt that the Lord was completely in control of my life. Since the beginning the devil has been trying to make God out to be a liar.

I just didn't understand it. Yet.

The truth was that giving everything over to an invisible God was incredibly hard to do. I was entrusting my life and that of my daughter to a God I could feel, but couldn't see. All I had was his word, his promises, his spirit, and other people who had known him and lived with him for a lot longer than I had. That was all I had to grow in my faith.

But it was all I needed.

I was telling God all the time how much I wanted to live by faith. I was saying, "God, if you want me to do music for you, you have to get me a manager to help me out." I didn't know how I was going to do the things he had told me to do. I just needed help.

Around that time, I got a call from an old friend named Z who used to hang out at a lot of the Korn shows. Now, like me, he had committed his life to Christ, and in his new Christian life, Z worked at a recording studio. He told me I should meet up with his boss, a guy named Steve Delaportas, who might be an interesting fit for me since I had been thinking so much about making music for God. I just knew I had to check this thing out because it felt like it might be a divine connection, so I talked to Steve and drove down to Burbank to meet him. When we met, he told me all about this vision God had given him for an entertainment company. I was hooked from the start.

passage to india

Steve's plan was an ambitious one, and it was made even more ambitious because it was all built around God. But there was more to it than just entertainment. Steve was also part of a ministry called Good News India that built orphanages for children in the poorest places of India. As he described the ministry, he told me that he would be traveling to India in a few months and, even though I had just met him, I told Steve that I would be coming too.

Meeting Steve was a tremendous sign, one that really showed me how God was continuing to shape and direct my life. Unbeknownst to Steve, I had recently been praying to God to show me how *he* views the world and to see the people that he would be with if he were here on Earth. I wanted to broaden my horizon and experience all kinds of people. Though I had traveled all over the world, I was always too drunk or high to appreciate it. When I heard about this India trip, I knew God was sending me to his people. Steve, however, had a much different reaction to the announcement that I was coming: he started laughing.

And laughing. He has one of those laughs where, once you get him going, he just won't stop. After he was through laughing, though, he agreed to let me come along. From that first meeting, I really dug Steve. It helped that he'd had a radical conversion like mine. He had terrorized the world, just as I had, before God yanked him out of that lifestyle, just like he had done with me. It took Steve a little while to quit trying to keep one foot in the world and one foot in Christ, but he eventually surrendered everything he had to God, which was around the time I met him. I could tell from our first conversation he had so much faith in God, and his faith drew me to him. When I saw his faith, it challenged me to trust God a lot more, and he also had more experience walking with the Lord, which helped me a lot.

The more Steve and I talked, the clearer it became that God really had brought us together because even though Steve had never managed an artist before, we both felt led, like God was calling him to be my manager. We prayed and fasted over it, and within a few days, we knew it was God.

Soon after that, Steve and I decided to become partners in ministry, and under this new partnership, our first order of business was India.

DISCUSSION QUESTIONS

1. Head discovered the spiritual gift of speaking in tongues. As he says, there's a lot of division in the church over this spiritual gift. Do you know anyone who's spoken in tongues? How do feel about Christians who do? Is it important to care one way or the other?

2. One of the unfortunate things Head learned early in his walk was that church denominations often contradict. How do you think your church compares to other churches? Would you visit (or even join) another church? Do you know any Christians who believe their denomination is the "right" one?

3. Head talks about how he eventually had a hard time at VBF because there were so many people there who were trying to help him in his walk. How big is your church? Do you like its size, or do you think it can be problematic?

4. After some time, Head gets to the point where he realizes that trusting in God isn't always easy. In what areas do you find it most difficult to trust God? What can you do to help your trust improve?

16. head-hunting in india

I felt the heart of Jesus the second I stepped off the plane in Mumbai, India. Almost immediately, we took to the streets and I was blown away by how many hungry people there were. It was heartbreaking. There were so many people in such desperate need, and I could not believe that more of us Americans were not reaching out to whelp. While we were sitting in luxury in America, these people were dying.

Everywhere I looked there were deathly skinny kids running around with no clothes. Thousands of them. All hungry. Walking by a mother with her son, someone gave them a bag of nuts or something like that, and they attacked it. I could tell it was the first food that either had eaten in a long, long time. I was shocked by what I saw, but I wasn't the only person; I had brought Jennea

People throughout the Loadi tribe were skeptical of us when we arrived, but even though their head-hunting weapons were threatening (especially to someone named Head), we persisted and won them over.

with me so that she too, could see how things really are in other parts of the world. As we went through the streets, the two of us were totally overwhelmed by the poverty and despair around us.

Shortly after we arrived in India, we started traveling around to the orphanages that Good News India ran. Before we left for India, God had moved on my heart to donate a certain amount of money toward these orphanages to help take care of these poor kids. When I told Steve how much I wanted to give, he told me I could just pay for a whole new orphanage, and after talking it over, we decided that it would be a good idea to open a new home to show all my fans where my heart now was.

We decided to name it Head Home, and I instantly got excited at the prospect of helping to ensure that these kids in India were taken care of by all these people who loved them. These kids were precious, and in need of our help. Like many Americans, I was totally in the dark about what these children faced, and the more I saw of India, the more I thought about how little we as a country were doing to solve this problem. Even though I hadn't been there long, I just knew that my outreach was going to be important.

another order from god

When the day came to visit my Head Home orphanage, it just so happened that it landed on June 19—my birthday. The problem was that because of the jet lag, I couldn't sleep the night before. At about four o'clock that morning, as I was lying there wide awake, I suddenly felt the Lord's presence hovering over me in my hotel room, just like I had that one time at my house. He was there, and I started weeping uncontrollably. His presence was just so thick—I couldn't contain it. Then I heard another direct order:

I'm sending you to the untouchables. Nobody wants them, but I do. Don't be afraid.

I had no idea what he meant, but I didn't care. I was freaking out because the Lord had just visited me, and I just wanted to do what he wanted. I got up, showered, got Jennea ready, and met the founder of Good News India, a guy named Faiz (who was an orphan in India as a boy—God rescued him, then sent him back after he had grown up to start this ministry), Steve, and our friend (and lawyer) Greg to go open my Head Home.

While we were waiting to leave, we got a phone call from this pastor named Tarroon, who was taking care of some of the kids in the orphanages. He said there was a certain tribe called the Loadi that had gotten ahold of him and said they wanted us to come to their village and talk to them about helping their kids.

The Loadi were a very a poor people, but there was something else: they were also murderous cannibals. We all agreed to go, because just before the phone call, I told everyone about that visitation I'd had from the Lord that morning, and the direct order he had given me.

It all made sense. Still, I thought, *But, Lord, these people might eat me!*

Anyway, we took off, and when we got to my Head Home, I saw all these great kids and their house mothers waiting for us. As we got out of the car, they did this parade/dance/song thing for us that was really cool and unexpected. After that, we saw where they lived, where they slept, and where they ate. We sang some songs to God with them and just had an unbelievable time.

meeting the loadi

But soon that time was over, and it was time to head into the jungle. Time to meet the Loadi. While I knew God was sending me to the untouchables, I didn't want to take any chances, so we left Jennea at the Head Home to play with all the other kids there.

We had already spent most of the day at the Head Home, and I hadn't been scared at all about visiting the Loadi—until we actually started driving to their village. It didn't help that one of the guys with us started talking in this worried voice, saying, "These people are ferocious headhunters!"

This was not exactly good news for someone named Head.

"If they want to kill us, let them kill us," Tarroon said with his big Indian smile. "Then we will be laughing with the Lord Jesus in heaven!" Then he started laughing joyfully at the thought of going to heaven.

I was quietly freaking out.

Now keep in mind that I had just gotten saved a few months before this trip, so as these guys were talking about all this, my eyes were bulging out of my head. Since I was saved, I hadn't second guessed anything that God had done for me, but this felt a bit extreme, not to mention dangerous. All I could think was that I couldn't die because Jennea was back at the orphanage waiting for me!

Suddenly all this doubt entered my mind. I started thinking that maybe that visitation I'd had that morning wasn't from the Lord—maybe it was the devil, tricking me to go there so I could get chopped up for stew on my birthday. As we drew closer to the village, I tried to shake that feeling, and luckily by the time we got there, I was fine.

Good thing, too, because there were about three thousand people there waiting to see us when we showed up. Wearing loincloths and body wraps over their skinny and malnourished frames, they stood there staring at us and asking how we were going to be able to help their kids. They were sick of seeing their children suffer and they wanted a better life for them, but they had no idea how to give it to them.

Right when we got out of the car, the man who seemed to be the leader of the group began talking to our interpreter, who translated for us. "He said if you don't help their kids like you say you will, they will hunt down Tarroon and kill him."

I found out later that some of these people used to raid Tarroon's orphanages, beat him up, and steal the children's food. Tarroon would never fight back, though. Instead, he would just tell them over and over that Jesus loved them, but still they continued to come back and steal things. These plundering trips had a strangely positive effect on them. On one hand they had been stealing, which was bad, but they had also seen firsthand that the conditions at the orphanage could help their kids. They knew that things could be better, and they wanted to reach out to us for help.

We started the meeting off by giving a little pitch about how we could help their kids. We were all pretty nervous, and one of the elders could tell. In an effort to calm us down, he spoke to our interpreter and said, "We don't even know the number of people we have killed. If we wanted to kill you, we already would have."

Comforting. I took it as the Lord's way of reminding me not to be afraid. Unfortunately, it wasn't really working too well.

As we spoke to them about what we could do to help, suddenly this drunk guy started shouting things at us. I didn't even know they had alcohol there, but it turned out that they make it from tree sap. (Sometimes wild elephants would come by and drink their alcohol, get drunk, and go crazy, ransacking the mud houses the people lived in, and sometimes even killing people.)

As the drunken man made a scene, our interpreter explained that the man was talking about how the Indian government had made the same promises that we were making but never came through. Because of this, they had to start eating people. They weren't savages—just hungry people.

The meeting ended with no more interruptions, so Steve, Faiz, Tarroon, and I started walking around their property to find a good place to build the orphanage. While we walked, the disruptive man followed us and continued to shout. To make things worse, he was carrying this big tool on his shoulder that they used for hunting. It was a club with a huge hook on it, sort of like a baseball bat with a hook on the part you hit the ball with. They use the club to kill their prey (animals or humans), then use the hook to drag them home. And now this guy was walking toward us. With his hunting club. It looked like things were going to get rough.

I started praying like crazy. "God, please change this guy's heart. Make his anger go away. You told me not to be afraid, but it's pretty hard right now."

He came closer and closer, and when he finally reached us, he paused for a moment, looked at us, then he burst into tears on Steve's shoulder. He started talking to the interpreter, who relayed his story to us.

"I have five daughters." He reached down, grabbed a handful of sand, and said, "This is all I have to feed them."

This was crazy. One minute, he was looking like he was going to attack us, and the next minute he was crying on Steve's shoulder, pouring out his heart to us.

God is so cool.

Well, we all started crying, of course, because we were just so touched by how much these people needed our help. Really, all they *needed* was love and help. That's it. After that, the presence of God just swept in and took care of everything. Seeing God in action like that changed my whole view on life, as I saw how he could bring about dramatic transformations in other people. It had been one thing when I watched God change my heart, but to watch him changing other people's hearts was dramatic. God had put a deep desire in my heart to help people.

The coolest thing was that in the time since we met the Loadi tribe, crime has dropped 90 percent, and today the orphanage is up and running in the Loadi village. Although we have since parted ways with Pastor Faiz and Good News India, that experience was something I will never forget.

By the time we left India, there was no question in my mind that the trip altered everything about my faith. Seeing the orphanages and helping the children of the Loadi people were incredible experiences that gave me this remarkable perspective on God and his plan for me—not to mention seeing God's faithfulness come through just in time when things were looking so dangerous.

The entire trip inspired me and my faith in God in such a profound way that when I got back to the States, I decided to do a little press to make people in America aware of what was going on over there. It was my feeling that perhaps the reason very few people were helping was because no one really knew the extent of the suffering there.

Unfortunately, this was not the case, and as I discovered not long after my return, many Americans didn't share my concerns. After I got back and spoke about India, I was still so high on my new life with Christ that I thought everyone I spoke to would want to jump on the first plane to go help them—like I did. Sadly, it wasn't so. But still that didn't change the experiences I had when I was there.

Ultimately God changed my heart during that trip, and like all things he does, it turned out that he had a reason. Once again, he was preparing me to turn my life in a totally new direction, and he wanted me to be as ready as possible for what lay in store.

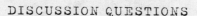

DISCUSSION QUESTIONS

1. Head visited India with Jennea to check out an orphanage that he donated money to create. Do you know the specific verse in scripture that talks about caring for orphans? If so, what is it? (Hint: It's in James in the New Testament.)

2. Have you ever participated in a short-term mission project? If not, what's been stopping you?

3. While in India, Head gets an order from God to go to the Loadi cannibal tribe. Have you ever felt God leading you to do something risky like that? Do you think its okay for other Christians to discourage such dangerous activities, even if they're for God's glory?

4. Head is right on when he shares that Americans, by and large, aren't too concerned with saving people in other nations. Where do you stand? If you are one of the concerned, what can you do to show it in tangible ways?

17. making music again—
god's way

When things settled down after my India trip, I took
some time to chill. It was summertime, so Jennea and I had fun
just hanging out together. Sometimes she would go over to her
nanny's house, but mostly we hung out together and had a great
time.

During these hot and lazy weeks, the Holy Spirit really started
empowering me to write more songs. The funny thing was that I
was feeling so much peace and love from God, I started writing
softer tunes because I just didn't have that same anger in me
like I used to when I was in Korn.

It didn't take long for that to change. One day, as I was writing, I felt the power of God's spirit fill me with passion and intensity, and I started screaming one of the songs I was working

It didn't take long for the Lord to lead me back to music.

on at the top of my lungs. After that day, I threw the idea of doing soft songs right out of my mind. It was clear that God wanted me to stay true to my passion for heavy music. I had been into metal and heavy music for as long as I could remember. Just because I was a Christian, it didn't mean I had to change what I was passionate about.

I was blown away at how the songs just flowed out of me. Up to that point in my life, I hadn't ever written full songs by myself. I had always had a band to write with, but God endowed me with more musical gifts than I'd ever had up to that point in my life. I was programming the drums, writing the bass and guitar parts, orchestrating the string and choir parts, writing the lyrics, and organizing the song arrangements. It was just amazing.

When I wasn't recording or hanging out with Jennea, I would head up to L.A. to talk to Steve. The more he and I spoke about my music and my situation, the more I came to see that God was setting me up for a move. Things in Bakersfield had been deteriorating for a while. Ever since I went public with my embrace of the Lord, it seemed like all my friends were either gossiping about me behind my back or trying to shove their noses into every part of my life. The whole situation irritated me.

In addition to these friend problems, God was sending me little signals that it was time for a change. One day when I was backing out of my garage, I noticed a bird that was trapped inside and flying in circles. Jennea and I got out of the car and tried to scare the bird out of the garage, but it kept flying from one corner to the next. We tried to free the bird for a long time but it didn't understand that the door was open for it to fly away. As I thought about the bird, the meaning of that sign from God quickly became clear. I'd been flying in circles for too long—I felt the Lord telling me that he was going to open a door for me to get out of Bako. Still though, I didn't understand how to go about it.

Steve and I bought a recording studio in Arizona, and through all of those things that were happening, I came to see that God was going to send me to the desert, just as he did with the Israelites in the Bible. He made them wander around the desert for forty years in preparation for the Promised Land, and while I didn't know how long I was going to be in the desert, I did know that God was going to send me there to prepare me for his calling and for my life's purpose. I just hoped it wasn't going to take forty years like it did for the Israelites.

After talking it over, Steve and I developed a plan: Jennea's nanny, Connie, would homeschool her while I went to Arizona for a few months, and every other week, Connie would bring Jennea out to Arizona to visit me. It seemed like a pretty good plan, but as it turned out, it wasn't God's plan.

so long, house

One day, while I was praying in Arizona, I felt the Lord telling me to get rid of everything in my house in Bako—except for the important things I needed—and then put my house up for sale. In addition, he wanted me to let go of all my friends from Bakersfield, even those friends from my old life who helped me become a Christian. It was his way of telling me to get rid of all the tangible memories of my past and say good-bye to the old Brian for good.

Part of God's message was that he didn't want me to go home at all before doing this, so I gave Connie a call and asked her to sell all my furniture and possessions. Then I called a realtor friend named Jeff and asked him to sell my house for me. They did it all. I never went back into that house after God told me to sell it. Connie boxed up the minimal amount of stuff I was keeping and put it in storage for me, while Jeff had my house cleaned and put it on the market.

This was a lot to give up all at once, but I fully trusted that the Lord was doing the right thing for me. Now I was not only changing my life, I was changing Jennea's as well. It was a big change and a hard one at that, so I asked the Lord to give me a sign—a buyer who would come very soon—to show me that he was in fact calling the shots. Later that week, the house sold for the exact price I wanted. The people who bought it fell in love with a lion statue I had in front of the house, and they had to have it. Not long after the closing, I spoke to Jeff, and he informed me that three days after my house sold, the market in Bako had a huge drop-off. If that's not a clear sign from God, I don't know what is.

wandering

It seemed indisputable that God *was* pushing me out of Bakersfield, but where was he leading me to? I knew God was real, and I kept seeing evidence of him, but even still, I struggled with a lot of disbelief and other difficult emotions. I had given up a lot in a very short amount of time, but not everything was easy. Periodically, my anger was still an issue and my depression was constantly looming in the distance.

I had known God for about six months, but walking with him was still really new to me. I loved this new life, but it was hard not knowing what I was doing all the time. It was hard to give up everything I had for him. Up to that point, I had spent my Christian life just running around everywhere, trying to do things for God, but I had been running around so much that I never really just sat and tried to enjoy him.

Now that I had the time for that, it was rewarding, but it was also scary because it showed me how much I had to learn about listening to God. I would pray and read my Bible, but I still felt like God was light years away sometimes. I didn't really have revelations yet that his Holy Spirit really did live inside me. I had read about it in the Bible and heard all these dudes preach about it, but I had a hard time believing it because I couldn't feel anything a lot of the time.

I was going all over the place looking for God, but all I really had to do was look inside. I had invited him in there, and ever since that's where he'd been—patiently waiting for me to understand that he would always be with me because he promises never to leave his children.

After I sold my house, I put all the important stuff that Connie didn't sell in storage and waited on God to tell me where to live. I told him I would live anywhere, and I meant it, since at that point, I was living in different hotels. In the end, I could only see two choices: California or Arizona. I really wanted to stick to Cali, so I looked everywhere in L.A., and I even tried to buy a house or two, but everywhere I looked, the doors were shut in my face. It was very discouraging, and I started a new kind of prayer; I like to call it freaking out on God.

"God, you told me to quit Korn!" I yelled. "You told me to go to Israel and India, and to sell my house. Why can't you tell me where to buy a house?"

It was frustrating for me because up until that point, I had felt God provide so much direction for me. Suddenly it felt like his words weren't in my head anymore, and I didn't know what to do. I finally got tired of the waiting and decided to go to Arizona and get a couple of rooms at the Best Western: one for me and Jennea, one for Connie. While Jennea spent her days homeschooling with Connie, I decided to head into the recording studio for the first time in a year. From the second I set foot in that Arizona recording studio, crazy things started happening.

While crazy stuff had always happened during Korn's recording sessions, there was nothing that could compare to this. Almost every day when I went in, entire songs would come pouring out of me: drums, bass, guitar, strings, choir, lyrics, everything. It was even crazier than before in Bako.

I was never able to write music like I did in that season. It was so clear that it was not me; I'd never had a recording experience like it. It was as if God was just downloading these songs inside me. At first, I wasn't sure where all of it was coming from, but as the songs came out I realized that many of them existed because recently I had spent so much time speaking with God in tongues.

tongues reemerge

Shortly before I went into the studio, I met a guy named Bob Cathers who was a pretty serious Christian. During our conversations, he taught me all about praying in tongues, suggesting that I pray for hours in tongues, because when you do that, you develop your ability to hear God more clearly in your spirit. I decided to give it a try because I figured that if it didn't work, I'd just stop.

Around that time, I had also started to reread *The Walk of the Spirit—The Walk of Power* by Dave Roberson a lot. On the whole, I still found the idea of praying in tongues really odd, but the scriptures can't lie, so I had to follow God's word and not my own thoughts and feelings. Believe me when I say it was hard. When you pray in tongues, you just sound like a babbling idiot at first, and since your mind doesn't understand what you're praying about (1 Cor. 14:14), you *really* start to think you're an idiot.

However, the Bible says that when you pray in tongues, you're edifying yourself (1 Cor. 14:4), building yourself up in your most holy faith (Jude 20), even though nobody—not even you—understands what you're saying except God (1 Cor. 14:2). I had to believe the Bible was true, because God can't lie (Heb. 6:18).

It took me a while, but by using tongues, I was able to build my faith and my ability to hear God, and because I chose to pray in tongues for so long, a lot of things in the spiritual world started to open up to me. The Bible started coming alive to me in a way I'd never experienced before. The sections in the Bible that were hard for me to believe just a few months before were starting to become very real.

One of the names of the Holy Spirit is the Spirit of truth, and through the tongues I was speaking, he was downloading the truth into my Spirit and crushing the "doubting Thomas" part of me. When I first was saved, the Bible felt more like an ancient book than something I could use to help my walk. Now it seemed like with every page God opened the door to my spiritual understanding wider and wider. Kind of like a door to another world.

By the time I went into the studio to record, praying in tongues was a regular part of my prayer routine and these doors were opening every day. Every morning, before I went into the studio, I spent around three hours with God, praying in tongues. When I finally got to the studio, the songs just fell out of me. It was uncontrollable and even started to happen when I wasn't in the studio. I would be in the middle of talking to someone, and God would just interrupt. He would speak to me right then, tell me to go to my computer, and write a song about what I had been discussing.

One time it happened during a conversation I was having with my friend Lisa. We were talking on the phone and she was in the process of explaining how she knew of a child who had a lot of problems and these problems were the parents' fault. Apparently they were kind of mean to the kid, they drank all the time, and they just didn't take care of their child as they should've (sort of how I used to be).

During our conversation, Lisa told me how it could be cool to write a song about kids rebelling against the negative things going on in their lives and running to God, so that he could bring healing into their lives like he did for me. After our conversation ended, I didn't think anything else of it until about twenty minutes later, when I heard this music in my head. It was heavy music. And then I heard the screaming words of the chorus:

Rebel!
Re-bel!
Your parents have failed you and I'm here to tell you
Rebel!
Re-bel!
The world has abused you and I'm here to choose you!

(Needless to say, I named the song "Rebel.")

I wasn't even trying to write a song; it just came to me so fast out of the blue. After I thought about it, there was no doubt in my mind that it was from God. The Lord spoke to me through Lisa, using her to trigger the idea for the song.

Something similar happened one morning when I was at breakfast with Steve, and out of nowhere, he said, "Bro, isn't it cool that we're washed by blood?" After breakfast, Steve dropped me off at my hotel, and suddenly, this music came into my head as it had after my phone call with Lisa. I heard the drum parts, the guitars, the strings, the chorus, the verse—everything.

This song was so catchy that I didn't have to go to my computer; I knew I would remember it when I went into the studio the next day. The chorus went like this:

Washed by blood
From deep inside

You're not a prisoner of your old life
Washed by blood
A brand new start
It's time that I rebuild your heart

So I named the song "Washed by Blood."

That wasn't the only song that came to me at my hotel room. One morning, I opened up the door and saw a newspaper lying on the ground. I picked it up, and that was the first time I saw New Orleans covered by the waters of Hurricane Katrina. Once again, I heard all the music, and then the lyrics for the song "New Orleans" came to me:

Bodies floating
In the streets of New Orleans
What does this mean?
Is the end coming?
People drowning
In the streets of New Orleans
What does this mean?
Is the end coming?

One by one, these lyrics came to me, sometimes in pieces, sometimes all at the same time. After I'd been writing for a bit, God gave me another song called "It's Time to See Religion Die." To me, this song has a few different meanings. For one, it encourages people to get out of the whole Sunday Christian mentality and into society so God can use them to change the world, to help people understand that God does not live in buildings made by men (Acts 7:48). We are God's building, because he dwells in us (1 Cor. 3:16).

Also, this song is for all the people who've been hurt by religion. All of the man-made religion in this world, Christian or not, has to die. It must grieve God's heart when Christians fight about whose doctrine is right; he doesn't see denominations, he sees one big glorious bride. When Christians argue about doctrinal issues, all he sees are people acting like children.

All that prideful, controlling religious garbage is what drives young people away from churches, and it has to go. Much of the world's population is under the age of eighteen, and we have to bring the love of Christ to them without trying to control them. Because where the spirit of the Lord is, there is freedom.

These lyrics in the chorus came to me rather quickly while I was in the studio one day. It's a throw-your-fist-in-the-air chant:

> *I testify*
> *It's time to see religion die*
> *The truth can't lie*
> *It's time to see religion die*
> *Who cares who's right?*
> *It's time to see religion die*
> *I'll crush the fight*
> *It's time to see religion die*

It is a powerful song and it really came from the heart because God is all about freedom.

Probably the most personal song—and the one that touches me the most—is called "Save Me from Myself," which is something of a roller-coaster ride from my drug use to my suicidal thoughts (with my demonic thoughts telling me to keep snorting more lines) to me crying out to God.

N.B.

The middle verse talks about me kicking all of my bad habits: drug use, abuse, depression, suicidal thoughts, and lying. And my favorite part of the song is when I'm screaming to God, thanking him for saving me from myself, and telling him that I'm through with me and am living for him now. The words *save me from myself* were exactly what I needed to scream to God

after everything I had gone through up to that point in my life.
Here are some lyrics from the verse and chorus:

Another day in life
Which way will I go?
Will I pick suicide?
How do I say no?
The demons are calling me
"Just one more line"
Voices echoing in my head
These thoughts aren't mine
Chop it, snort it
The kid? Ignore it
Life sucks, I'm over it
Save me from myself
Can't quit, I tried it
Your love? Denied it.
Can't fake it
I hate it
Please help me
God, save me from myself
I'm begging you
God, save me from my hell

For a while, I was going through this songwriting phase where
I wrote almost a song a day for a couple months, and then, just
like that. . . it stopped. I've tried to write songs a few times since
then, but I just can't do it; to me, that's just another confirma-
tion God was working and living through me, empowering me
to write songs with his Holy Spirit.

After the writing process was over, I ended up with about
three albums worth of material. While I was writing those
songs, we had a guy named Josh Freese come in to record the
drum tracks on some of them. Josh isn't a Christian, but he is a

great drummer—maybe the best studio drummer around right now (he's played with A Perfect Circle and Nine Inch Nails and appeared on about two hundred albums).

Anyway, he came in and slammed through my songs, making these beats I wrote sound awesome. A lot of times, I was still writing songs when he had finished recording, and I really wanted him to stay because he was such a help to the process. He used to joke about me, saying, "I'll be pulling out of the parking lot, on my way to the airport, and there's Head chasing me down the street, holding his guitar and screaming, 'Come back! Don't go! I have another song!'" The truth was that he played a key role in my finding a sound for all those songs. He was a huge blessing.

But after my run of songwriting, my depression and anger returned. When I recorded my guitar tracks, my temper really acted up sometimes. I was short with the engineers and sometimes yelled at them. I didn't really want to, but I had no self-control—so I had frustration to deal with too. But in spite of myself, I had fun tracking those guitars. I hadn't recorded guitar properly since Korn made *Untouchables*. It was nice recording with a sober mind.

DISCUSSION QUESTIONS

1. In this chapter, Head shares that God told him one day, out of the blue, to sell his house—and not even go back into it. And Head did exactly what God said. Have you ever heard from God in that way? If so, how did you respond?

2. Head talks about a new prayer he started learning— freaking out on God. Do you think God minds if we freak out on him?

3. Head writes about how he felt God's presence calling him to write songs and how he felt God making him a better musician and writer than ever before. Have you ever felt God making you better at something?

4. One of Head's new songs is titled, "It's Time to See Religion Die." In your mind, what are the negative things about religion? Is there a difference between someone who is religious and someone who is spiritual?

18. dreams and visions

Around the time I was recording these songs, I had my first of many vivid, prophetic dreams from God. Throughout the Bible there are many stories of God speaking to people through dreams. One of the main reasons he speaks to us in dreams is so he can speak straight to our hearts. There are so many dreams floating around every night, but every time I've gotten a dream from God, I've known it as soon as I woke up. And from the moment I woke up after this dream, I knew it wasn't ordinary; it was from God. It was incredibly vivid, almost like a movie (like that vision in the plane before I became a Christian).

In this dream, I was with Steve and Jennea in a weird building. Suddenly, I noticed an elevator, and Steve jumped onto the outside of it and held on tightly as it started going up. When Steve started going up, I left Jennea by herself and jumped

---

Coming out of the darkness has been hard, but over time I've learned the walk of faith.

up toward Steve, grabbing onto his legs. So Steve and I were going up this elevator, on the outside, dangling. We reached the first story of the building, stopped for what seemed like a few seconds, and then we kept going.

And I started to get scared.

Looking up, I saw that this elevator went *way* high into the sky, disappearing into the clouds. It was clear that I had a long trip ahead of me and I held on for dear life because the longer the trip got, the farther the fall would be. The elevator stopped on every floor, so it took us awhile to reach the top, but when we got there, we were so high that we were in the clouds.

Once we arrived at the top floor, the elevator started going back down very fast. This part of the trip seemed much more dangerous than going up had, but I wasn't afraid. It was actually kind of fun, like a roller coaster, or like one of those death drop rides at an amusement park.

When we reached the bottom, I started looking around for Jennea, but I couldn't find her. Somebody told me that she was very upset that I left her, so she ran away.

I was terrified. I started looking all over that weird building for her, but she wasn't anywhere to be found. She was gone, and my heart was broken.

That's when I woke up.

I didn't understand the entire meaning of the dream all at once, but over the next couple of months, God revealed it to me. As I came to understand, the dream represented the wild adventure that God was going to take us on. He made it clear that, because we were walking completely by faith, it would be difficult and a little scary at first. But it was our job to just hold on tightly to God and trust him completely.

Each floor we reached as we ascended represented a different level of spiritual growth and understanding that we would receive while walking with God. At the same time, our vertical movement demonstrated how we progressed away from our old ways of doing things, such as trusting in ourselves. We had a lot of pride to get rid of. The achievement of reaching the sky symbolized us reaching enough maturity in Christ that God would release us to his purposes, and then we would go back into the world to bring people close to the Lord too.

But there was another crucial message that God wanted to get through to me. At the time I had the dream, I had been working nonstop on my new music. Connie was pretty much taking care of Jennea full time, and I hadn't seen her much. I hadn't even realized that was happening until the dream. In it the Lord showed me how I was leaving Jennea out of my new life with God, the same way I had left her out when I was with Korn. So here I was, doing the same thing with her that I had done before, and God was showing me that Jennea might resent me later in life if I kept pushing her to the side.

Even though I didn't understand every piece of the dream right when I woke up, one thing was clear: I had to spend more time with Jennea. I prayed about it, and within a week, I decided to let Connie go and focus on my relationship with my daughter.

When I realized the power and the clarity of this dream, it made me think more about other dreams that I had in the past that seemed particularly vivid. During my time with Korn, I had a dream that reoccurred several times over the course of my ten years in the band, and although I didn't know it then, it turned out to be a dream from God.

In the dream, I was hanging with my friends, drinking and doing stuff that wasn't productive for my life. Then, suddenly, I would get really panicked and run home to my parents as fast as I could because I realized I was still in high school and I hadn't done any of my homework all year long, which meant I wasn't going to graduate. When I realized what I had done, I felt like a huge failure. It depressed me. Then I woke up and still felt like a huge, depressing failure. I was disturbed every time I had that dream, but I always wrote it off as nothing more than a dream.

After I got saved, God showed me that *he* had been behind that dream, and that he was trying to send me a message that I was wasting my life. He was trying to show me that if I kept it up, one day it would be too late—I wouldn't graduate into eternity with him. Yet another sign from God.

God doesn't make the choice for us—he wants us to choose on our own to live for him. In that dream, he showed me that my fame and fortune wasn't going to get me anywhere—I had to choose him.

There's a reason I shared this dream with you. I believe a lot of people—maybe even you—are having God-given prophetic dreams and don't know it. Just like I was. Since those dreams are from God, only the Spirit of God can reveal the true meaning of them. So ask God to reveal to you any dreams from your past that you may have missed. See what he shows you. Because he just might be trying to tell you something.

But it's up to you to listen.

vision wisdom

It took me awhile to understand that dreams were a totally different way to understand God, and I learned that from other people I met along the way who knew about dreams. After we'd been working together for a bit, Steve introduced me to his friend Benjamin Arde who had amazingly prophetic gifts. He was thirty-one years old at the time, but he had the wisdom of someone who had been around much, much longer. God called him at a very young age, and he has been living for him ever since.

When I talked to Benjamin, he would tell me about some of the things he had seen, and he always had the coolest stuff happen to him. He had some visions of heaven, and he had a lot of experiences where he saw angels. Jesus even visited Ben once or twice in a vision. I used to joke with him and say, "When is the Lord gonna start giving *me* more visions, Ben? When am I gonna be able to see angels, dog?" He's South African, and he would just say very smoothly, with that accent, "Brian, Brian, Brian. In due time, my friend."

I'm still working on my visions, but Benjamin really does hear from God. He'll tell us about things that are going to happen in our lives before they actually do. One time he even told Steve and me that God was going to replace everyone in our company in the next eight months. Sure enough, eight months later, most of the employees had quit or had been replaced.

Another time, after I finished writing and recording my songs, Ben prayed with me and the Lord showed him that I was going to go through a period of really dying to my old self. God was going to uproot some painful things from my past and replace them with new roots—stronger roots of peace, happiness, confidence, and boldness.

I was excited to hear that these roots would be stronger, but he also had some less encouraging news: before those new roots could be planted, I was going to go through a lot of pain while God dug up all the bad stuff in my past. To complete my healing process, I was really going to learn what the cross was all about. I was going to have to learn how to suffer for Christ. As Ben explained, it's very beneficial to go through the cross of Christ to get rid of all the pain, bitterness, jealousy, anger, depression, abuse, and all the ungodly things we have accumulated over the years. God showed Ben that I was going to just sit there and go through deep pain a lot of that time. But it wouldn't happen all at once; it would be in stages. And it would all help me in a huge way.

Not long after that, I met a man named Kim Clement, who is nationally known for his prophetic gift and is shown all kinds of crazy things by God before they happen. When I sat down with Kim, he explained to me that he had some visions about how God was going to use me to help kids know the true walk with Christ, not the religious walk that pushes so many kids away from God. I didn't know exactly what he meant, but I trusted his vision and continued exploring with him and other people.

I also learned a lot from a guy named Lance Wallnau who had a prophetic gift too. When I sat down to talk with Lance, he heard something about me from God that I didn't really like at first. He felt like God was telling him that it would be very healing for me to go to my dad and talk with him about my childhood—about his anger, and how it affected me.

The only problem was that I didn't want to do it. I tried to tell myself all that stuff was in the past. I thought it was all "under the blood," as we say, and I couldn't really see what good it would do. I guess my fear of confrontation was trying to kick in again.

I decided to check this prophecy out through God, and I started praying, asking him if it was for real. Well, actually, I said, "I don't want to do this, Lord. I'll probably just start crying and make an idiot of myself. I'm a grown man. I don't want to bring up the past."

After I finished complaining to God, telling him what was up, I felt like he said:

Go to the computer and buy an airline ticket to Bakers- field to talk to your parents about your childhood.

Don't be afraid; I will be with you.

I felt the presence of the Holy Spirit all over me, and I was already weeping uncontrollably. I knew it was another direct order from God himself. He showed me that even though my sins were washed away by Jesus' blood, I still had a hard time with forgiveness and suffered from bitterness issues in my heart. The Lord wanted to set me free, but there were steps I had to go through to get that freedom. Understanding what I had to do, I bought the plane ticket.

time to talk

A week later, I arrived in Bako and went straight to my parents' house. On the morning of the day I was planning to talk to them, I prayed.

"Lord, since you're making me do this, please at least help me not to make a big scene in front of my parents. I'm thirty-five years old. Help me do this like a man."

On that day, I learned another big lesson about God's faithfulness. Not only was he with me, but it wasn't a big scene at all. In my mind, I had made it out to be this huge, scary thing to do, but it ended up being really easy. I told my dad how his anger had affected me when I was a boy, and that it had continued to affect me my whole life.

Sitting there across from him, I explained how whenever someone raised their voice to me, I would get a similar feeling that I felt when I was a boy and he had gotten angry with me. I also told him that when I was a boy, I had felt like something was wrong with me because of his anger. I told him I felt like I hadn't been a good enough son to him. I just laid it all out there.

My dad apologized for everything he had done back then and told me he loved me very much. He explained how he had problems in his own life that he didn't know how to deal with because his own dad had done the same things to him when *he* was a kid. That anger was a curse that had been repeating itself in all the generations of our family.

Now that chain was broken. By accepting Christ into our family (which my parents did—when I got saved, they started checking out a church to see what I'd gotten into and wound up accepting Christ), the curse was over. We were talking about the anger and exposing the lies we had all believed about each other. Those lies had no power anymore. It was like God entered our lives and Satan had to leave. The light of Christ exposed all the darkness.

My mom also apologized for whatever she felt she had to, and then I apologized to both of them for all the junk I put them through, like holding bitterness against them inside me for all those years. We all instantly felt like a load was lifted off us; just like that—it was over. And it only took a few minutes. From that conversation on, we have been closer than we ever were before. Similarly, my brother Geoff and I are closer than ever too. It's amazing how the Lord can restore a family so quickly.

a new home

All this stuff was happening around the same time: Connie leaving, recording my guitar tracks, and Lance giving me this prophecy. And that whole time, I was renting this little apartment (we had only stayed in the hotel rooms until we found this place), because I didn't know where the Lord was leading me to live.

A couple weeks after my elevator dream, Steve came over to my apartment and said, "Come on, God's gonna give you your house today." I hadn't even been looking for a house, and plus, God didn't let me know where I was going to buy a house—why would he tell Steve? But I was bored, so I went to look with him, figuring it might be fun.

The first place we went to was cool, but it wasn't my style. Also, it cost three million dollars. I wasn't going to spend any-where close to that. If I was going to get a house, I didn't need something huge; I just wanted something to fit Jennea and me.

We wound up at this house right next to a mountain, and I felt the Lord say that it was mine. It was like, "Surprise! Here's your house!" I didn't get too excited, though. I just figured if it was meant to be mine, it would be mine. The sellers ended up accepting my offer, and not long after the closing, I met them.

It turned out they were Christians who had been praying for someone who loved God to buy the house. They loved that house and didn't want to turn it over to someone who wouldn't take care of it, and they were overjoyed at the prospect of us living there.

About a month later, Jennea and I were living in a house again, rebuilding our lives together, by ourselves. We had a blast decorating the rooms and watching our furniture come in, slowly but surely. And I had a great time being a full-time dad, like I was supposed to be. For the first time in a long time, I wasn't relying on my parents or a nanny to watch my kid. Just as God had shown me with the elevator dream, I needed to be involved in everything about her life. God was right, and I felt so good. Almost all the time it was just me taking care of her: cooking breakfast, making dinner, building my relationship with my daughter and God, taking care of her, taking care of me, and basking in the life that God had led me to.

money, money, money

While I was in the process of buying the house, I had some other financial issues occupying my attention. The biggest was a legal dispute with Korn over money I thought they owed me as a founding member.

But soon after I got lawyers involved, God put an end to it, telling me to drop my suspicions, not to stir up any more bitterness with the band, and that he was going to take care of me from now on. What could I say? I had to listen to God.

By this time, in addition to our new home, I had spent a lot of money on my new recording studio and on paying for my engineers and other personnel. I also felt moved to give some extravagant gifts to different Christian ministries, which was hard for me at first. I had spent years of my life thinking that all those Christian places rip people off (and I'm sure a few of them do).

But God sees everything, and he will judge everyone according to what they do, including me. My job is not to question, but to do what the Lord says and cheerfully give the money he tells me to give. If I do that, he'll reward me for my obedience.

Giving money to people and ministries when God tells you to is very important to him. He knows that we work hard to make that money; he knows how much money can mean to us, because most of us spend more time at work than we do at home with our families. As you give whatever amount the Lord tells you to give, you're showing him that you trust him to take care of your needs. You're showing him that money is not your god. When you give money away, you make it clear that you believe in heavenly rewards, not earthly ones—and God sees this. He sees where you put your faith. When you give, he sees how much you give as well as the attitude you give it with, and he ends up giving you back more than you gave anyway.

I had always hated the feeling of being poor—like back before Korn, when I sold those stolen drum machines to make ends meet. I hated that feeling, I hated stealing, and I hated being broke. So when I got rich, I was determined never to be poor again. I had to keep making as much money as I could, so I saved a lot of the money I made in Korn, and invested a lot of it too. I resolved to have a big fat bank account forever so I would never have to worry about money again. I could never have enough. I always needed more.

It was an obsession, and I was a slave to it.

So you can imagine how I felt once I was out of Korn and my bank account started getting lower and lower after buying my house, recording equipment, and giving money away. I really had to start learning about God's provision, because I was panicking.

I said, "God, look at my bank account! I gotta pay my mortgage! I gotta take care of my kid! This is lower than I've seen it in ten years! Please fill it back up! I gave a bunch of money to those ministries, like you told me to! Where's the return?"

Of course, God was testing my faith and trust in him. He was showing me that he was all I needed. He was letting my bank account get to the point where I *really needed* more money in it to live. It wasn't just a mental, greed thing where I just wanted more money. At that point, I *really* needed more.

And God did provide for me just like He promised.

From that, I learned that money comes from wherever the Lord sends it. He pays me, not anyone else. I can't even tell you how much this flipped my mind. Totally renewed it. God set me free from greed and worry. Because worrying about money is a huge problem for a lot of people. It's stressful. It was for me.

Since that day, I try not to worry about money or anything else anymore. Besides, Jesus says in Matthew 6:25–34 not to worry about our lives. The Lord will take care of us. He wants everyone to live a stress-free, worry-free life.

reconciling with korn

I had made peace with my parents and rid myself from my dependence on money. I had taken every step that God had told me to take, but there was still one more crucial thing to do. I had spoken to a few of my bandmates since I left Korn, but not all of them. Shortly after I was saved, David called me and told me he was proud of what I did, which was a great show of support that really made me feel good.

A few months later, Fieldy's dad passed away, and I went to the funeral. While I was there, I saw Fieldy, and we had a chance to make our peace.

But that funeral had pretty much been my last contact. A long time had passed since I had spoken with Jonathan, since we had exchanged so many nasty words in the press. When I got ahold of him, I apologized for all the stupid stuff I had said, and he did the same. It was awesome. Short, but to the point.

Similarly I had not really spoken to Munky since I left the band, which was always something I'd felt bad about. When I left Korn, I was pretty sure Munky felt like I had left him hanging the most. He and I were tight, since we did all the guitars together and we were generally the two peacemakers in the group.

Around the time I called Jonathan, I also sent Munky a few e-mails, apologizing for leaving the way I did. He wrote me back saying that he loved me and forgave me. That made me feel really good, because I really missed him when I quit.

Taking those steps was difficult, but really important for me to let go of my past. I needed them to know how I felt about leaving and how I could have done things differently—especially in the aftermath. From talking to all of them and to other people, I've heard that those four guys were closer than ever after I left. In the end, I guess the shock of my departure pulled them together. I'm happy about that, and I'm glad that they're doing so well.

DISCUSSION QUESTIONS

1. Have you ever sensed that God was speaking to you through a dream—or even through someone else's

dream about you? If so, did you do anything as a result of those dreams? What was the outcome?

2. One of the visions that was shared with Head involved him going to see his parents and telling them how their behavior toward him growing up negatively affected him. Head went through with the visit, and it actually worked out fine. Is there anything you want to share with your parents? If so, how difficult will it be to carry out this task? How do you think they would respond to you?

3. Head talks about being set free from his love of money— a tough job for someone who had so much of it! What object or habit are you looking to free yourself from that could be difficult to let go?

4. Head writes about the importance of listening to God when it comes to giving money. What are other ways, besides money, that you can give back to other people in the name of God? Does your youth group do any volunteer outreach? How can you get involved?

5. After all the difficulty with the band and with Head's leaving, he reached out to each member to make peace. Have you ever felt God push you to make up with any of your friends who you've fought with? Is there anyone right now that God wants you to make peace with?

19. breakthrough

Once I made peace with my parents and Korn, I felt I was ready to go into the studio and lay down some vocals to the songs I had written. However, it didn't take long for me to realize that singing was going to be a lot harder than I'd planned.

Before I got saved, I was pretty insecure about my voice, but I hid it behind drugs and alcohol. Now that I was sober, I didn't have very much confidence in singing my own songs. As the recording sessions progressed, this frustration with my voice **N.B.** didn't go away. I was trying so hard to get the performances down that I stopped letting God do it through me. I had forgotten that this whole thing wasn't supposed to be about me. I was still trying to be the rock star, and I had to learn that this music wasn't coming from me, it was coming from God. I was merely his instrument.

God and Jennea are the center of my world. Everything I do, I do for them.

It didn't help that a particular dark, heavy cloud of depression that had been in and out of my life for a while was coming back to me in a big way. Though I had felt my depression looming on the horizon for months ever since I was saved, it had yet to really affect my life on a day-to-day basis. But I should have known that it was only a matter of time, and as it turned out, the vocal tracks did a lot to push me back into darkness and doubt.

In the beginning of recording my vocals, I was overflowing with anger, which made it incredibly difficult to get anything done. Sometimes I would just completely lose it and smash the computer keyboard that controlled the recording while I was doing my vocals. Other times, I would go home and cuss God out a little. Often the depression got so intense that I felt like I wanted to give up. I felt like I had been abandoned, like I was on my own again, and I could feel the darkness of my earlier life closing in on me.

The vocal tracks made me question myself, and once I started questioning myself, I questioned everything else—including God. I was living the prophecy that Benjamin had given me about completely dying to myself, and it was incredibly difficult. What made it even harder was the fact that I was so confused and disillusioned I didn't even remember the Lord warned me about all of this stuff when he gave me the prophecy.

All I could focus on was my intense depression. My soul was in complete darkness, and I could barely see God at all. I couldn't understand what was going on with me.

raw in front of the lord

That was a very hard time in my walk with God, but I didn't give up. I didn't understand what was happening to me so I had to learn to completely trust God. I was so used to being totally numb that I didn't know how to deal with the raw pain I was feeling and asking God to help me through was totally new to me.

One day, I felt so much pain and torment in my soul that I totally lost it and started screaming at God.

"I hate you!"

"Get away from me, get out of my life, and leave me alone!"

"I thought I got saved!"

"Why are you letting me go through this torture?"

I didn't know what I was saying. I didn't know what I was feeling. I didn't even know what I was thinking. But even after I said those things to God, I felt him smiling down on me, gently trying to help me understand that I had done a lot of damage to myself over the years, and it was going to take some time to heal those wounds.

The Lord knew it was going to be hard for me to change into the person he wanted me to be because I was so used to living the total opposite. Even after I'd been following the Lord for several months, there were still attitudes and ideas that I had not totally parted ways with. There were still things that he needed to change about me. He had a lot of pain and other junk to squeeze out of me, and believe me—when that stuff leaves you, sometimes it screams at God on the way out. And when the pain from your past leaves you, sometimes you have to feel it again as it leaves.

The good news is that there is nothing we can say or do that will separate us from the Lord's love. I was really bummed out after yelling at God like that, but the truth is, when I accepted Christ, God became my heavenly Father. And if one day Jennea came up to me and screamed at me like that, I would still love her the same. And God still loves me the same. Those hard times really made me thankful that the blood of Jesus covered all my sins and that God would never count them against me.

Those rough weeks of deep depression brought out the worst in me. Besides yelling at God, I would be mean to Jennea. I would think about doing drugs, and sometimes I would even wish I were dead. There were so many nights that I would have bad dreams in which I would go back to Korn on drugs, while everyone laughed at me, saying, "I knew he wouldn't last as a Christian."

Perhaps the most frustrating thing about all of this was that I couldn't control any of it and I couldn't find my faith in God like I had in the beginning. I was going through the things that Benjamin had prophesied for me, but I had absolutely no power over them. It was harder than I could have ever imagined.

To this day, I still don't understand everything that went on during those times, or what it was all about, but I remember feeling like God was really mad at me. Now I know that it had nothing to do with God being mad at me, but back then I used to wonder why he wouldn't just heal me. I was so confused. Was he testing me to see if I would go back to my old ways? I wasn't sure.

pleading my case

I cried and cried. I pledged to God to never to go back into the world. I begged for mercy.

"God, please stop this pain and depression. I'm sorry for everything I've ever done in my life! Please take this away!"

Anything I could think of, I apologized for. I tried making a list of everyone I had hurt and everyone who had hurt me, and I would cry out to God.

"God! I forgive so-and-so!"

"God! I'm sorry I hurt so-and-so!"

"God, I thought I was your son! I wouldn't let Jennea go through this; why are you letting me?"

And then it would go away for a week, but it would soon come back.

But then one day I finally realized that screaming at God and begging him to take away my pain wasn't going work. So I completely surrendered myself and stopped fighting him, and I asked him what he wanted me to do.

And for the first time in a while I got a response to my question.

He said:

Just worship me. Praise me and worship me through the pain.

And that's what I did. I cried and worshiped the Lord in stillness and silence, listening to worship music and lying on the ground in his presence. It was time for God to do all the work, and it was time for me to be quiet. That's what got me through those dark times.

tears of pain, tears of joy

Because God inhabits the praises of his people (Ps. 22:3), he was right there with me the whole time. He taught me that the only thing I needed to do was be still and quiet while the pain surfaced, and then I could just cry it away. Usually the pain would surface when I was at home worshipping God, but there were times that it would surface while I was out and about in the middle of my daily routines.

For instance, I would be driving with Jennea in the car, and I would feel the pain rising and tears would come pouring out of my eyes. But I would cry quietly, hiding my face from her so I wouldn't upset her.

Or I'd be in the studio and I would have to step into the restroom to have a good cry. Other times I found myself in public restroom stalls crying for a while too.

I would get pretty annoyed when that stuff happened because I felt like a basket case, but I learned to remain silent and not complain to God because I knew that every tear I cried meant more healing for me.

All of that crying and the mood swings were really difficult during that season, and through it all I tried to remind myself that this whole thing was necessary. God helped me by showing me that the divine light of his Spirit was shining in my soul, burning away all of the junk from my past and replacing it with the wisdom of his unconditional love—which was exactly what I needed in my soul—love.

As an illustration, he reminded me of what it felt like to walk out of a movie theater in the middle of the day after sitting in the dark for a couple hours. Walking out into the sunlight, my eyes would burn until I covered them up with my hand. He told me that the light of his presence, which he was shining in my soul, was a similar light, and this was another reason I was feeling so much pain.

He also reminded me about all the different people in the Bible who fell to the ground with fear and trembling when they came into the Lord's presence. That understanding completely floored me. I spent so much time screaming at God, or rebuking the devil, when in reality, it was the light of the Holy Spirit that was purging my soul from the impurities so I could be in complete union with God. That understanding made me fall in love with him even more.

But that was not the only encouragement he gave me; the Lord also said some other things that helped me deal with my suffering. He reminded me of all the pain he suffered when he was on the cross and how he offered up all of his suffering to his father out of love for him and for us. He showed me that I could offer my pain and suffering to the father in the same way he did.

I was so comforted with those words, and they continue to comfort me to this day, and whenever I feel bad now, it makes the pain much easier to deal with because everything I do now is out of love for God.

christianity is no easy ride— but it's the best one!

I've had some of the best times of my life since I became a Christian. I've also been through some of the hardest times of my life. But I'm sure it wasn't easy for the Lord to get hung on a cross either, and his Holy Spirit will strengthen me with the same courage and endurance as the Lord Jesus had in my time of need.

Those times of worship and fellowship have brought me incredibly close to the heart of the Lord. They made me realize that I can get through anything with him by my side. As time went on, that heavy depression I had been battling for years finally went away; God completely took it out of me just like all the other things he set me free from. He replaced all those roots of anger and depression with roots of peace and happiness. But I still have bad days just like everybody else. They're not anywhere near as bad as they used to be, but they're still there.

In the Christian life, things are not all perfect like some people say they are. It's kind of like the different seasons of the year. One season you can be seeing, feeling, touching heaven, having all kinds of real encounters with the Lord and feeling higher than you ever imagined you could feel. The next season you might feel so spiritually dry that you're going to crack.

But I've learned that the spiritual droughts are just as important for my spiritual growth as the times when I'm touching heaven. It all teaches me to walk by my faith in God's love, not by my circumstances, feelings, or by what I see. The Bible is very clear that Christians are called to be blessed by God, but we're also called to pick up our own crosses and suffer for our faith sometimes too. The coolest thing is after we endure our seasons of suffering obediently, God promises that more of Christ's power will rest on us (2 Cor. 12:9–10).

In the end, it's all been worth it because God is very real and I can get through anything and everything I have to in this life, good or bad, because God loves me, and I love God.

Period.

And on top of all that, I can look in the mirror every day and smile because I know that giving my life to Christ was the best decision I ever could have made for Jennea and me.

I shared a lot of the details from my past because I wanted to show you how much of a monster I was for a reason. I lied, I cheated, I stole, I abused my wife, I was a horrible father—I was a closet criminal, and the guilt and shame were eating me alive, but I chose to share those horrible things to prove to you that Christ can and will clear anyone's conscience from any evil act. He did it for me, and he will do it for anyone who comes to him (Matt. 11:28).

I went through a lot of junk to get back to where I belonged, but finally after a lot of work, I'm there. And my main prayer for this book is that it encourages you to seek after a deep and intimate relationship with God.

Take it from me: nothing you chase after on this earth will satisfy you like a real, everyday, intimate relationship with Christ.

Nothing.

Trust me.

While I was in Korn, I had people waiting on me left and right. Anything I wanted, I got. Anywhere I wanted to go, I went. All I had to do was give the word and it happened.

I had the world in the palm of my hand, and I have to tell you one last time: *there's nothing there.* I promise you.

Jesus Christ is the only one who can make you complete.

That's it. That's the end of my story.

Well, on second thought, it's actually only the beginning because my life is just getting started . . .

DISCUSSION QUESTIONS

1. Head learns that becoming a Christian doesn't mean all your pains and troubles automatically go away. Quite the opposite—he learned that he still had to deal with his depression and anger issues. What sorts of things are you still dealing with from your past now that you're a Christian?

2. When Head got raw before the Lord in his pain, it wasn't an easy thing to go through—in some ways it was similar to the drug withdrawals he endured in the past. But God brought healing to him in the end. If you're dealing with unresolved pain in your life, are you willing to get "raw" before the Lord and let him heal you, even if it hurts?

3. After Head gave in and stopped trying to prevent the pain from happening, God's work on him really began— and many, many tears were falling from his eyes. What can we learn from this? When is the last time you let yourself cry before God?

4. When someone like Head—who once had every luxury and advantage the world had to offer—becomes a Christian and proclaims that there's "nothing there" in the vast sea of worldliness he was swimming in, how does that make you feel about your decision to follow Jesus?

epilogue

Have you ever loved someone so much that you would die for that person? I'm talking about a love so strong that you would do absolutely anything for that person? Maybe it's one of your parents, or your brother or sister. Maybe it's a boyfriend, girlfriend, or your spouse. You would do *anything* to keep that person safe, protected, and out of danger.

That's how much God loves us. His love for us is so deep and passionate—so much deeper than anything we can give to our own loved ones (Rom. 8:38–39). God proved that love to us when he sent his only son Jesus Christ to die a horrible death, instead of us, so that justice would be done and so that we could be reconciled to God through the crucifixion of Christ.

If you ask Christ to be your Savior, you're basically saying, "God, thank you for not punishing me. Jesus, thank you for taking my punishment on yourself." It is an awesome miracle, but that should only be the beginning. Sadly, a lot of people stop right there and go on living for themselves, and while they might be saved and are going to heaven, they don't experience the riches of God's fullness in their lives.

Those riches from the eternal realm of heaven are available to us now as we live on earth. We don't have to wait until we die. God will let you experience heaven. All you have to do is ask and keep asking him.

See, the blood of Christ covers all our ungodliness so that we can go to God boldly in prayer to ask him questions, or just hang out and talk to him like a friend. And that prayer, that first prayer, is something precious. It is a time when God comes so close to you that, if you're willing, he sends his Holy Spirit to live inside of you.

The Holy Spirit is the same spirit that raised Jesus from the dead, and he's the same spirit that took away all the pain in my life. He is very real. The Holy Spirit is God himself, living in you, speaking to you, listening to you, and showing you how to live this life to its fullest.

He set me free from a broken heart, a broken soul, and a broken spirit; from drug addiction, alcoholism, guilt, shame, abuse, anger, depression, confusion, and on and on. He'll do the same for you if you let him in. A simple, sincere prayer from your heart to God is all it takes to start you on your own road to freedom. A prayer like this:

God, in the name of Jesus Christ, I want to thank you for sending your Son to die in my place. Please forgive me for my past, and help me to believe and trust in Christ. God, please send your Holy Spirit to live in my heart, to teach me how to know you. Thank you. Amen.

That's it. I cut the prayer short, just to give you an example, but you can keep praying for as long as you like, because if you pray in the name of Jesus, I promise you—God is listening. But please don't feel pressured to say that prayer or anything like it. I had to come to a point in my life when I decided to be the one to say this prayer, not anyone else. Remember how I said it with Eric, and then took it back when I got home? It's because I needed to come to that decision on my own.

I'm not trying to force you into anything here. I don't want you to say this prayer just to say it. My hope is that if you say it, you'll *mean* it; that it will be a sincere prayer to God, straight from *your* heart.

Once you say it and mean it, all that's left is to pour your heart out to God. Ask him to reveal himself to you. Ask him to baptize you with his Holy Spirit. Ask him to open up heaven to give you a glimpse, because he has invited you (Rev. 4:1). Ask him anything you want. "Because anyone who comes to him must believe that he exists and that he rewards those who earnestly seek him" (Heb. 11:6).

Talk to him like a friend, every day, as much as you can, and he will reveal himself to you. Because now you are a friend, and a child of God.

God bless you.

acknowledgments

I've never written anything in my life, unless you count the school research papers I did to keep my teachers and parents off my back, so I have to give all the credit to God for the books I've written.

Thank you, Father, for inviting me into your heart and showing me the reality of your paradise, and for your unfailing, unconditional love. Thank you for sending your Son Jesus Christ to die in my place. Thank you, Lord, for saving me from myself. Thank you for turning all things around for good, and thank you for using me as one of your vessels.

I gotta thank my kid for putting up with her dad while he was going through the roller coaster of emotions—baby girl, God has set Daddy free, and you'll never see that scary guy I used to be again.

Wait up, I gotta thank God again for sending me a couple of guys who could help me make sense of all the scrambled memories from my past, and those guys are Adam Palmer and

Jeff Dunn—you're amazing. There's no way I could've done this book without you guys. You were truly handpicked by God for my book. Adam, thank you for all your sleepless nights and your time away from your family (but you're the one who waited until the last minute).

Matt Harper and everyone at Harper Collins—thank you for believing in me and helping me get my story out to many people who are in pain. Dave Urbanski—thank you for all the editing, bro.

I also want to thank my family and all of my friends I've ever had in my life, past and present. Especially the ones who went through difficult times with me and stuck by me even though I didn't deserve it: Mom, Dad, and Geoff; Rebekah—I'm truly sorry for everything I put you through while we were together; Korn—thank you for allowing me to share the good times and the bad times we had together; D—thank you for helping me get off drugs; Kevin, Terry, and the rest of the Amadas—thank you for showing me how to ask Christ into my heart when I was a boy; Benjamin Arde; Ron & Debbie and everyone at VBF; Eddie and Jenae and everyone at Grace; Rex, Jay, Christian, Steve, Doug, Sandy and family, Eric, Sheryll and family, Doug Bennett, Joey, Moses, Connie, and Nathan—thank you for helping me get to know Christ.

I want to thank my friend Lisa, who encouraged me to write this book, even though I wasn't very excited about it at first because writing wasn't one of my specialties. Lisa—you have no idea how writing this book has helped set me free. God has used this book to empty out all the guilt, pain, and shame from my past. Thank you for hearing God and pushing us all to get this book where it needed to be.

I gotta say thanks to my business/ministry partner, Steve Delaportas, for going to battle for me. Man, I know for sure that a lot of people would have quit if they had to go through what you go through. Thanks for not giving up.

Thank you to my friend and lawyer, Greg Shanaberger, for inspiring me to keep going with this book when I thought it ended at my salvation. Some of the best parts of this book are the ones you encouraged me to write.

I want to say a special thanks to all of my fans who stuck by me and didn't ridicule me for my decision to give my life to Christ. Your faithfulness helped me get through a lot of dark times.

I gotta give a shout of thanks to the Montoyas and everyone at Ruby's Tattoo. You guys are all truly amazing and humble artists.

I also want to say thanks to my engineer and friend Carlos Castro. I really appreciate you putting up with my spiritual growing pains, man.

There have been a lot of ministries I would like to thank that have helped me grow in my walk with God: Benjamin Arde Ministries; Jay and Christian at the Sanctuary in Huntington Beach; Joyce Meyer Ministries; Todd Bentley with Fresh Fire Ministries; Bob Cathers; Kim Clement; Lance Wallnau; Dave Roberson; Patricia King with Extreme Prophetic; Rick Joyner; God TV; www.elijahlist.com; Graham Cook.

I've done thank yous on seven albums with Korn, and I always forgot to thank some people, so I know that I'm forgetting some people right now. I want to cover myself now, so thank you to all the people I forgot to thank.

Okay, that's everyone.